AND THE NIGHT IS SPANGLED WITH FRESH STARS

AND THE NIGHT IS SPANGLED WITH FRESH STARS

A STORY OF ETERNAL LOVE

by Claire Russell

"There is no remedy for love but to love more."

Henry David Thoreau

© 2018 Claire Russell - All rights reserved.
ISBN: 9780964296824

Dedication

To my son Alex who cleared the path.

To my son Adrian who lit the way.

To Chris who pointed me in the right direction.
To Jill who stood by me until I could stand alone.
To Stuart Weeks who saw a testament in me
and encouraged me to write it.
To Todd, the one who "got it".

To Bronson Alcott, for friendship, for companionship, for the kiss you gave to Henry on his deathbed.

To Louisa May Alcott who wrote the poem "Thoreau's Flute" in memoriam. She simply loved him.

To Ellery Channing, favorite walking companion who loved Henry with a deep and constant affection,

And to Henry David, beyond the beyond the beyond, ever and anon.

To John Henry, David Charles, James Devereaux, Edmund Sewall, Cynthia Rebecca, Annie Alcott, our beloved children who never were but should have been. They live in our hearts.

Word to the Reader

There is a flower known to botanists, one of the same genus with our summer plant called "Life-Everlasting," a Gnaphalium like that, which grows on the most inaccessible cliffs of the Tyrolese mountains, where the chamois dare hardly venture, and which the hunter, tempted by its beauty, and by his love, (for it is immensely valued by the Swiss maidens,) climbs the cliffs to gather, and is sometimes found dead at the foot, with the flower in his hand. It is called by botanists the Gnaphalium leontopodium, but by the Swiss Edelweisse, which signifies Noble Purity.

Thoreau seemed to me living in the hope to gather this plant, which belonged to him of right. The scale on which his studies proceeded was so large as to require longevity, and we were the less prepared for his sudden disappearance. The country knows not yet, or in the least part, how great a son it has lost. It seems an injury that he should leave in the midst of his broken task, which none else can finish,—a kind of indignity to so noble a soul, that it should depart out of Nature before yet he has been really shown to his peers for what he is.

But he, at least, is content. His soul was made for the noblest society; he had in a short life exhausted the capabilities of this world; wherever there is knowledge, wherever there is virtue, wherever there is beauty, he will find a home.

This concluding passage from Emerson's eulogy to Henry David Thoreau brought to an end the offering (talk), **The Henry David Thoreau We Do Not Yet Know**, that I gave in Concord's Masonic Lodge at the July, 2017 bicentennial anniversary celebration of Henry David's birth.

The offering was drawn from a book, 33 years in its unfolding, that I had completed earlier that summer. The book, **"Says I to Myself: Thoreau's Seminal Science of the Spirit**, spoke of Henry David as pioneering a path of knowledge that leads the spirit in man — for those who can imagine — to the spirit in the universe. Like unto like, simply expressed for the moment. Deep calls upon deep.

In my Thoreau bicentennial offering, I referred to Henry David's own experiences along the path of knowledge of, in his own words, the "mystic, transcendentalist, and natural philosopher to boot."

Specifically, I introduced the terms: clairvoyance/clear-seeing, clair-audience/clear-hearing, and clairsentience/clear-sensing. That offering is printed in the postscript of this testament that you hold in your hands. For it provides a context for this story. **As its author notes, such labors are, above all,** *labors of love.*

As I was gathering up my notes at the conclusion of my talk in the Masonic Lodge, a striking woman from the audience walked up to me, someone whose presence had caught my eye while I was talking. Pausing, she took a breath and looked at me deeply before speaking:

"I understood what you said." (About Henry David's clair-voyance, clair-audience, clair-sentience, his *common* sense.)

She paused, continued: "And Henry David understood what you said."

Our gazes met . . . . and then she was overcome with tears.

I reached my hand out to hers and held it quietly for a few moments before asking: "Do you care to say more?"

That *Claire* (herself) did.

Much this friend shared in the final days of the bicentennial celebration about her life and that of Henry David's. That account is the delicate "stuff" of this testament. Of particular note with respect to this "Word to the Reader" was Claire's statement, which prompted our meeting:

"I recall well, Stuart, needing to approach you, compelled by a gentle nudge between my shoulder blades from an invisible hand... that, I believe, has guided me over my life times."

Can it be, friends, that there is, indeed, more to life than meets the eye? That is, there's what we refer to solidly as the "real world." And then there is the *real* real world — that world that may reveal itself to be truer than life, that life that we have come thus far to know, accustom ourselves to?

The encounter took place, as noted, in Henry David's home town, Concord, Massachusetts: *"I was born in the most estimable place in all the world,"* he wrote in his journal, December 6, 1856, *"and in the very nick of time, too."*

Can you imagine, friends, that what makes Concord "inestimable," as Henry David suggests, is that its history is woven, indeed forged, of veritable revolutionary-transcendental realities, miracles themselves "heard 'round the world".

Can it be that testaments, such as this one that you hold in your hand, allows us to meet Henry David Thoreau on, as expressed, his own *clear* and *spirited* "transcendentalist" terms?

As you proceed through these pages, I invite you to keep in heart and mind Henry David's well-known passage about building our castles in the air, "that is where they should be." Indeed, may this very testament provide, at long last, the opportunity, as Concord's native son goes on to say, to "put the foundations under them."

That said, let me add, and emphasize, that the following words of mine, and Claire's, are bound, friends, to be challenging in our modern age saturated with what is referred to as "materialism." Challenging — can one add? — even for those "kindred spirits" of a Thoreauvian, transcendentalist bent.

How so?

Louisa May's words aside, Henry was human, as I trust you, his devotees, can understand? If not readily appreciate? That is, as a mortal, an incarnated human being, Henry had a shadow, which he cast… on himself and at times on others around him. Human he was. In *A Week on the Concord and Merrimack Rivers,* he offered the following reflection with respect to such a shadow and what it, in turn, reflects…. its origin:

"Every man casts a shadow; not his body only, but his imperfectly

mingled spirit. This is his grief. Let him turn which way he will, it falls opposite to the sun; short at noon, long at eve. Did you never see it...?"

That is, for Thoreauvian devotees, Henry is, indeed, a hero, *imperfect*. As a matter of fact in his imperfections — if we can/will imagine? — we may discover his greatest heroics.

His beloved friend, Waldo (Emerson) himself struggled with this realization, that is Henry's imperfections — not to mention Emerson's own, his aspiring humanity. In the eulogy Waldo was asked to give at Henry's service — the service of his junior, his dear younger friend, who had journeyed on to the beat of his own drummer — in that heart-wrenching task Waldo gave voice to the following words:

" *'I love Henry,' said one of his friends, but I cannot like him; and, as for taking his arm, I should as soon think of taking the arm of an elm tree."*

[Those words and the eulogy itself, I have sought to mend/amend — on both Henry's and Waldo's account — at the completion of the testament, noted, 33 years in its unfolding, " **'Says I to Myself': Thoreau's Seminal Science of the Spirit"**.]

The point, friends...?

If we are human, mortal, if, that is, we are here on earth as incarnated souls, we have a shadow. Which, as noted, we inevitably cast... on ourself and others?

Henry *was* human, mortal, incarnated here in Concord, one of the most transcendental/ miraculous places on earth. That is, Henry David Thoreau had a shadow.

No where perhaps is this better expressed than in his own words, which one prominent Thoreauvian was able only to dismiss, i.e. question its interpretation, even attribution. Henry David Thoreau would not utter such words, this good soul proclaimed:

"It is wonderful, wonderful," you noted, Henry David, in your Journal of Dec. 20, 1851, *"the unceasing demand that Christendom* makes on you that you speak from a moral* point of view. Though you*

be a babe, the cry is, Repent, repent! The Christian world will not admit that a man has a just perception of any truth, unless at the same time he cries, "Lord be merciful to me a sinner."

[* Such a passage out of the mouth of the subject of this "testament," Henry David Thoreau himself, asks for some explanation. Toward that end, Concord's native son elaborates in his journals and in "A Week": *"I have met few men who have a genius for Christianity"*... *"Nothing will dignify and elevate science when it is sundered so wholly from the moral life of its devotee."*]

Carrying on our delicate thread, such words regarding repentance and sin will, understandably, have little meaning for many readers — apart for the millions upon millions of fellow citizens of all religions, faiths, aspirations who've encountered this land's quintessential, i.e. "All-American," wisdom. I speak of that wisdom which has been duly exported the world around, including, if my recollection serves me rightly, the over 13,000 such fellowships in one rather small country alone, Iran.) I refer to the 12 step fellowships that began with alcohol and that now embrace pretty much every obsession (in our thought life), craving (in our feeling life) and compulsion (in the life of our will) — every addiction, that is, on this blessed earth of ours.

To repeat, friends, so that this essential point is clear: Henry David's words about repentance and sin will, understandably, have little meaning — apart, as noted, for the *millions upon millions* of fellow citizens of ALL religions, faiths, aspirations who've encountered this land's quintessential ("All-American") wisdom, which has been exported the world around... *if, if,* that is, those millions in the fellowships have taken those 12 steps seriously, above all, as regards this "testament," Step 4 itself:

"We made a searching and fearless moral inventory of ourselves."

In the light of such inventories, this blessed "reckoning" about Henry David Thoreau will not only make sense, but, I trust, friends, that it will kindle/rekindle our spirits, Transcendental or otherwise. For Henry David took (and in these pages takes) such an inventory of, and for, himself. *And he was/is chastened thereby.* Indeed, in such labors of love lies, I do believe, his quintessential genius, his humanity. If we can imagine…? I do trust.

~ ~ ~

Gathering up the strands of our thread, this "testament" is more than hero worship. It is, as expressed, a testament, a labor of love… eternal love.

Don't bother (yourselves) to read on, unless you're prepared to meet not only this "mystic, transcendentalist, and natural philosopher to boot," but unless you're prepared to encounter this lover of dear Ellen Sewell (truth be told) *and* through Ellen, through this aspiring "testament," to meet a lover of humankind.

If the foregoing is clear and there is a moral to this story, it is the fact that Ellen, her Self, embraced Henry in his fullness, shadow and all. That fact is the undying "promise" of love, a love that is borne of compassion, *com-passion*, our ability to *suffer-with* the other.

Toward that aspiring end, friends, I draw this opening word, Word to the Reader, towards its conclusion with a reflection that, I hope, serves you along your way in this story.

That is, if questions arise as you proceed with this testament, I invite you to return to the following seven considerations that bare witness, I believe, to Henry David's life, death, and his ongoing existence:

1) In physics we speak of the forces of attraction. If such forces propel a presumably dead, inanimate universe, what do we imagine these forces of attraction can set in motion in the living, animated, human realm?

2) Specifically, how is our connection with someone, once near and dear, who has laid aside his or her physical body (i.e. died) different than it is with someone, still alive, with whom we also feel a deep bond — though the person is out of sight, dwelling, for instance, on the other side of the globe?

3) Otherwise expressed, what is it that we love about another? Anything beyond their physical, visible body alone, their "mortal coil"?

4) If so, when a person dies, need that *non* physical love, that loving connection also pass away? Or, might we be attesting to more than we imagine when we note, for instance, that someone who "passed away" (their physical body, that is) "came to mind," is "in my thoughts"?

[On a more personal note, my dear mother's response to such a question was an illuminating one — with respect to those in the retirement community where she and my   father live: "Ma, how many of your lady friends have felt the presence of their husbands after they had passed away, bodily: 30%, 40%, 50%?" Ma's response, without a moment's pause, remains a memorable one: "Over 90%."

Can it be, over 9 ladies out of 10 stay in touch with the departed ones, their beloved? Can it be, friends, that we know more than we understand (consciously); that our task is to come to *understand* ever more fully what we *know* (unconsciously)... about this wide world in which we find ourselves?]

Carrying on with our golden thread:

5) If such love, such connections do *not* simply pass away, how do we keep them alive — kindle that holy flame of the heart?

6) The foregoing question may take on an added meaning if, upon the death of the person "we have in mind," he or she bore in their heart a great sorrow or other deeply held feelings. Do we imagine, that is, that such feelings immediately disappear, vanish on the other side of the threshold now that one has arrived in heaven, (if not less idyllic realms)? Is it as simple as that? Or, might circumstances come to mind when the sorrow, the feelings spoken of live on... as they do for many upon awakening from sleep to the old/new day? Sleep, the little sister of death? While such grace (a new beginning) certainly exists, is it guaranteed? Or, in certain circumstances, might something *more* be asked of us?

7) Finally, this is the story, the testament of Henry David Thoreau's long-lost, and, if you can imagine, newly-found love. That is, it is a love story, the story, as noted, of eternal love. As such, these pages offer as human an account of Henry David as one may have ever found, if not

sought, or imagined: the Henry David Thoreau we do not yet know. All the nearer and dearer to our hearts?

For those who *are* able to imagine that such humanity may abide within Concord's native son — *"I ask to be melted."* You confided to your journal, Henry, on April 11, 1852. *"You can only ask of the metals that they be tender to the fire that melts them. To naught else can they be tender."* — for those so inclined we come to the consideration that lies at the heart of this testament that unfolds before you. Might there be something that we here on earth can do to lessen the loads of those we continue to love, who live on in other realms... such as Henry David Thoreau himself?

Emerson's words come to mind as I write, the glimpse of an exchange with a visitor who extolled Plato and Socrates "with gravity":

> *"I bore it long and then told him that was a song for others, not him. I told him to shut his eyes and let his thoughts run into reverie or withersoever -- and then take an observation. He would find that the current went outward from man, not to man. Consciousness was upstream."*

If this 7th and final consideration, along with those that preceded it, make sense (common/uncommon sense), I offer a picture that may serve to make the "testament" that follows more comprehensible.

Imagine yourself on a l o n g long distance, wireless phone call — that is the connection is made with the smallest of devices tucked all but out of sight behind your ear.

Is the picture clear, to begin with?

You are sitting at your desk, for instance, talking with someone you can't see, someone, as noted, who could be all the way around the world... or, if you're the family member of an astronaut, you are talking with someone in outer space itself. As expressed, the person you're speaking with is invisible — *but you can hear them*. If the connection is a good one, and you're alert, the communication is made.

The subject of this testament, Henry David Thoreau, spoke to just such a possibility in his perennial best-seller, *Walden* — with a key caveat that addresses the moral, so to speak, of this story, story of eternal love. Each word that follows bears volumes, above all in and for *our* time?

> *We must learn to reawaken and to keep ourselves awake, not by mechanical aids, but by an infinite expectation of the dawn, which does not forsake us in our soundest sleep. I know of no more encouraging fact than the un-questionable ability of man to elevate his life* [and that of others?] *by conscious endeavor. It is something to be able to paint a particular picture, and so make a few objects beautiful; but it is far more glorious to carve and paint the very atmosphere and medium through which we look, which morally we can do.*

Stuart Sinclair Weeks, Founder
The Center for American Studies
Concord, Massachusetts, USA

P.S. Henry David's own words of introduction to this testament follow, both past and present. If one can imagine? Of note is the fact that Concord's "native son" is not the only fellow mortal/immortal who, as expressed, recognized that there is more to both life, and to death, than meets the (outer) eye — to say the least. Indeed, there is a literature, as old as the ages, that speaks to such "transcendental" realities. As may become clear in the following pages, this story of eternal love might prove to represent a new "departure," or, better said, a new arrival, a new and dawning chapter in this perennial philosophy. That is, it offers those with eyes to see a novel and — may it be? — an engaging angle of vision on its subject, one of the most widely read and researched figures of our age: a Henry David Thoreau that we may not yet know… his very heart of hearts.

Acknowledgments

I acknowledge with deepest respect the descendants of the Ellen Sewall and the Joseph Osgood families who share a legacy that is timeless and enduring. I am honored to be able to present this testament to you as a current addition to Louise Osgood Koopman's, "The Thoreau Romance.", written by Ellen Sewall's daughter.

It was your book, Robert Sullivan, "The Thoreau You Don't Know," that helped me find a starting point for my journey. "The Book," I call it, which I discovered in a bargain book catalogue. My story about finding Henry again truly begins here.

Walter Harding and Robert Richardson, your biographies inspired me to read more about Henry Thoreau. Walter, sadly, you are no longer with us, but you were a large part of the inspiration that kept me moving forward on my quest.

When I inquired about a biographer who focused on Henry the mystic as opposed to natural philosopher and political activist I was directed to Alan Hodder's book "Ecstatic Witness" where I found the mystical Henry, the one who "got it."

Corinne H. Smith, whose "Westward I Go Free" is an important and ambitious account of Henry' trip westward to recover his failing health. You did the legwork, and through your wonderful book I got to go along for the ride.

Laura Dassow Walls. Thank you for a new biography of Henry. It is eloquent and poetic.

My last thoughts go to the men I consider our own Founding Fathers of the Thoreau Society, the men who kept Henry Thoreau's name alive in the mind and hearts of men. S. A. Jones, A.W. Hosmer, H.S. Salt, and Kenneth Walter Cameron. The debt of gratitude that I feel for you and the painstaking work you've done on behalf of Henry Thoreau to keep him alive and in our consciousness is endless.

- Claire Russell

"Methinks my present experience is nothing; my past experience is all in all. I think that no experience, which I have today comes up to, or is comparable, with the experiences of my boyhood. And not only this is true, but as far back as I can remember I have unconsciously referred to the experience of a previous state of existence. "For life is a forgetting," Formerly, methought, nature developed as I developed, and grew up with me. My life was ecstasy. In youth, before I lost any of my senses, I can remember that I was all alive, and inhabited my body with inexpressible satisfaction; both its weariness and its refreshment were sweet to me.

This earth was the most glorious musical instrument, and I was an audience to its strains. To have such sweet impressions made on us, such ecstasies begotten of the breezes! I can remember how I was astonished. I said to myself – I said to others – "There comes into my mind such indescribable, infinite, all-absorbing, divine, heavenly pleasure, a sense of elevation and expansion, and [I] have had naught to do with it. I perceive that I am dealt with by superior powers. This is a pleasure, a joy, an existence, which I have not procured myself. I speak as a witness on the stand, and tell what I have perceived."

The morning and the evening were sweet to me, and I led a life aloof from society of men. I wondered if a mortal had ever known what I knew. I looked in books for some recognition of a kindred experience, but, strange to say, I found none. Indeed, I was slow to discover that other men had had this experience, for it had been possible to read books and to associate with men on other grounds. The maker of me was improving me. When I detected this interference I was profoundly moved. For years I marched as to a music in comparison with which the military music of the streets is noise and discord. I was daily intoxicated, and yet no man could call me intemperate. With all your science can you tell me how it is, and whence it is, that light comes into the soul?"

-- Henry David Thoreau July 16,1861

> *"I could say with the poet,*
> *"Sweet falls the summer air*
> *Over her frame who sails with me;*
>
> *Her way like that is beautifully free,*
> *Her nature far more rare,*
> *And is her constant heart of virgin purity."*
>
> Henry David Thoreau, July 1840

"The other day I rowed free , even lovely young lady, and, as I plied the oars, she sat in the and there was nothing but she between me and the sky. -- Henry David Thoreau, June 1840

"I have always loved her. I have always loved her".
Henry's last words about Ellen when he heard her name mentioned by his sister Sophia when he was on his deathbed. -- Early May, 1862

*****

I know the author of this book well, as you will see, as deeply, as intimately as I know myself. She is a part of me and so I can make that claim. She has shared with me what she has written, and I have added a few of my own words when asked to do so. The words she has written about me, about us, will stand. This is her story, about a significant part of her life that she has chosen to speak about and as difficult as it was to share it, for she has kept what she has written private until now, she has done so. With all my heart I offer this testament to you in her name. -- Henry David Thoreau

All of my life I have believed in the sacredness of fact, the obligation that each one of us must speak the truth by stating the

factual account of things, the real, rather than the unreal, what is true as opposed to what is untrue or fiction.

My real life began in Concord, Massachusetts when I fell in love with Ellen Sewall. She was the lodestar around which my life revolved. All that I did I consulted her first in my heart before acting. All that I wrote I shared with her in my thoughts before setting words to paper. Did I consider marriage to someone else when I lost her to another man because we were forbidden to marry? No. I lived alone, with the woman that I loved, in my heart.

What I am about to say matters a great deal to me and I hope that it will be perfectly clear. To all of you who have written books about me, studying my life, my thoughts, my feelings, and believe perchance that you know me from the research you have done, even trying to gain clues about me from my own writing I say this: You think you know the deepest parts of me and have written what you have discovered in your books. You might believe you have finally unlocked the secrets and broken the code that reveals who I am, but if you have failed to see the gift of Ellen Sewall in my life and how loving her helped determine the man that I was, you have missed much. For she is most of that deepest part of me, part of that very code that you search for, of who I was and who I am and it was right before your eyes.

I must say this as well, for it is an answer to the universal question that is sought by everyone at some time in their life, when they are ready to ask it: Love began with the divine breath that quickened the life force within us. It is that vitality that drives us, that compels us to seek, that leaves us incomplete if we do not find that part of us that is missing from our very selves.

Our hearts are bereft without that divine complement, the only one who can speak our personal language and knows our name. The love that lives in our hearts will flicker and die without the recognition and acknowledgement of the existence of that Other who is separate and yet one with us, made of the very same essence that makes us one to one, each to each.

Ellen and I are the divine complements of which I speak, filling the voids in each other, bringing us to wholeness. It is the requirement of the universal quest for fulfillment to find that particular love, which we both understood as a divine imperative, to move heaven and earth if need be to complete the journey and thus to ensure that the indwelling divine spark of love will never die but live forever, the spark that will remain an eternal flame. So it is with Ellen Sewall and me. For all of you who seek your eternal beloveds, may you also find them. -- Henry Thoreau

~ ~ ~

What you are about to read is my story, but it could be yours as well, the passing of your beloved husband or wife or significant other, not Henry David Thoreau who is part of my story, but the person you are eternally connected to, with hearts and souls that recognize each other though you dwell in different but complementary worlds.

This story is for all of you who have experienced this divine phenomenon that is so extraordinary it cannot be adequately expressed with words. But, I speak as well to those of you who are conflicted about what to believe regarding love that exists after death, a love that is expressed and shared with the beloved who remains here on earth. I invite you to simply consider what I and so many others have experienced and continue to do so and that your hearts and minds remain open to something that is incredible but exists within the realm of possibility.

As the words you are about to read suggest, eternal love can live, even thrive after death, beyond physical time and space, and so hearts that were once connected in life can remain so, for no boundaries exist to keep them apart.

Our earthly world is connected to the heavenly world by the thinnest of veils. And the love that manifested these worlds was meant to be acknowledged, recognized and shared by all of us. I have found it to be so, and so I share my story with you. It begins when I was a child. For that is the starting place for most of the stories that we tell ourselves and others who care to listen.

~ ~ ~

When I was very young, no older than three or four, I discovered a link between my world, (which at that time meant my house and my yards, back and front) and the sky, the heavenly world, the place where the stars lived and the sun and moon, too.

I had no words to express what I had discovered, but I knew it to be true, for I felt someone or something was calling me, trying to reach out to me from somewhere far away, somewhere beyond my world and the people I knew who lived in it. I listened every night as I lay in my little bed and heard words coming from somewhere and fell asleep to star visions and the subtle songs of the universe.

I am long past the age of three or four. Others, who have lived before me, long before, and will come after I am gone, have heard and will hear *their* songs, that recount how the worlds in our universe are connected, as one beloved is connected to another. But my little girl self knew nothing of those things at the time. I just knew that there was another place, not just the house on Grant Ave. where I lived with my mom and dad and older brother, but someplace bigger, undefined and undefinable to my child's mind. What I *did* know was that wherever *it* was, was real because I felt it. Whatever it was, the feelings I got about it, made me feel safe like I did when I was in my dad's strong arms or when mom tucked me into bed at night, singing a lullaby to put me to sleep. It was love I was feeling, as simple and as complex as that, but love that is immeasurable, infinite, the love that birthed us all by the creators great and continual act of creation. What I got from my parents, what I gave them was multiplied countless times, and I felt it and knew it to be true.

~ ~ ~

Imagine, if you will, that you are three years old and you have the vocabulary of a child that age, so that you cannot articulate with words what you experience, not even to the people who love and know you best. When you look at something, anything that catches your eye, you feel that you "know" it, you "feel" it, what it's like to be whatever it is that you see. It is almost as if you *become* that tree, that telephone pole, that house, that bird, and you also know what it feels like to be the person who captures your attention. You become "one" with people and things, so much so that your world is complex in a different way from the world of most children, frightening in inexplicable ways, threats sometimes perceived because something doesn't feel "quite right" but with many good and wondrous experiences as well. And these things, these experiences, are not perceived with your physical senses but are just as real to you as if they were.

I still remember an incident very clearly that occurred when I was very young, about that age of three. I was at the home of my paternal grandparents and they were entertaining a young man whom my parents and I had never met. He was trying to be agreeable and show how well he could relate to a small child, so he pretended to "steal my nose". I became hysterical and would not be consoled, even after he showed me that my "nose " was his thumb. Not even reassurances from my mother that my nose was, indeed, still on my face could ease my fears.

Of course he did not steal my nose, but to me he seemed incomprehensibly mean. Why would he even pretend to do such a terrible thing? Why did he think I would find it amusing? The fear I had felt was replaced by anger. I also felt the man's feelings all the while, confidence at first, that he had shown everyone how he could amuse a young child, then confusion when I became hysterical, then his own anger at me for refusing to be consoled. That was one of the incidents that was not so pleasant, and it had a lasting impact because I still remember it so clearly today.

Most often there were what I refer to as the "opening up" times. For instance when I connected to things like a flower or a tree or grass or snow and to people with kind hearts, gentle spirits like my parents and my friends. I felt safe and filled with joy and wonder at the world and people around me. One of those times happened on the way back home after visiting my cousins with my mom and brother. It was springtime, March or early April and we took a back road home to the city, quite a few miles from where we lived. Not far from my aunt and uncle's farm we passed a large hill covered with crocuses that were so dense that the hill was completely saturated with the color purple, all shades of it from the palest lavender to the darkest royal blue.

Nothing else was visible except that color and those early blooming delicate flowers spread out upon that hill for all to see on that lonely country road. The ecstasy I felt and wonder of it dazzled me and lingered as I felt myself filled up with the hill and the color of those purple crocuses. I felt saturated, *inundated* with the overwhelming sensations of crocus and color that I internalized, a feeling that lasted for days.

I didn't realize until I was much older that I saw my world differently than most people, that everything I experienced had more complexity. Everything and everyone I came into contact with was more nuanced as I perceived them with more than just physical senses.

I will explain to those who may be unfamiliar what the terms clairsentience, clairvoyance and clairaudience mean. They are simply ways of perceiving people and things beyond the realm of ordinary perception with our physical senses.

This is what clairsentience is like for me, which I have given some examples of already. It is the feeling of being a part of someone or something, even people that I don't know or things I have never seen before. What I am feeling with my physical senses becomes a link that connects me to what *cannot* be perceived with those physical senses. It is a *feeling* kind of knowingness, without accompanying sound or sight.

"Are we not one?" the heart asks. "Are we not that table in the corner, and stars also, and moons and planets?" No matter what form we take, human, plant, stones, water, dirt, we are one, we are kin and we can be a part of each other, through the gift of clairsentience.

Seeing with "spirit eyes," hearing with "spirit ears" is what I call clairvoyance and clairaudience respectively. When I see an individual who is disembodied, that is, someone who has left the physical plane through death and no longer inhabits a body, I am seeing *clairvoyantly* with my *spirit eyes*. If I hear a message from someone, words or sounds that I know I am not hearing with my physical ears, this is what is called clairaudience, hearing with *spirit ears*. It is also true that I often experience all three "clairs" simultaneously. Without exception I can feel clairsentience, but often with both clairaudience and clairvoyance as well.

These gifts of the spirit were part of me and so were brought with me into my adult life, experiences that were part of my life when I was a child. When I grew up and left home, which most of us do eventually, I worked for ten years as a data entry clerk, unfulfilled and dissatisfied, knowing that I could be doing something to help people rather than sit behind a desk all day in front of a computer screen.

Everything took an unexpected turn in the right direction when I met a man at a wellness center where my brother worked. He had studied and perfected a practice that he called "attunement", a modality that brought a dysfunctional endocrine system back into balance, as well as other healing practices that helped facilitate the removal of energy blockages from the entire body. I studied with him for two years and at the end of that time, with my mentor's blessing, I was now ready to set up my own practice. I began the most challenging, rewarding time of my life.

As I became more confident and my practice grew, disembodied individuals began to appear in the room, a friend or family member of the client I was working with at the time. Suddenly I would become aware of a presence in the room and I would see him or her, standing silently in the corner, very respectful of the healing work that was in progress, usually just observing, curious. Occasionally I was asked to pass along a message to my client which I did, if he or she were willing to hear it.

The presence of these spirit beings brought a complementary element of healing to my client. With the release of blocked energies from the physical body that I was able to facilitate and a reconnection of the client to the presence of a loved one who lives in a different world watching the healing process, a deeper result was obtained to the satisfaction of the client, to me as practitioner, and to the loved one who stepped across the threshold from one world to another to bring that much welcomed additional positive energy to it all.

Beings from the angelic realms would also appear, sometimes to assist in the healing work that I was doing, but I most often saw them standing at attention, immobile, vigilant and watchful, to guard and protect the client and me from dark or negative energy that could have entered the room and would have compromised the healing space.

Going back to what I said earlier in this narrative, words can be heard and/or felt through the gifts of clairaudience and clairsentience. Loved ones can be seen clairvoyantly. They may come from a different world than ours now, but they come across the bridge that love made, that we created with them, heart to heart that connects our world and theirs. Love made the bridge, love keeps it strong and enduring, as strong as the bond we forged with them when they were here with us on earth and continues to exist, invincible, undeniable, from our world to theirs, from theirs to ours, neverending, eternal.

Here then, is my love story. It is a love story about a village called Concord in the state of Massachusetts and also for a person from a different time, who lived there.

~ ~ ~

"We'll go to Concord before we return to Wisconsin." Dad said. "We shouldn't miss it as long as we're in Massachusetts. There are two places I particularly want to see while we're here. The Orchard House where the Alcott family lived and Ralph Waldo Emerson's house".

' Anything to keep us here longer,' I think to myself. I dread the miles that take me away from here, for I have just spent the best summer of my life at my aunt and uncle's house in Boxford and I am not ready to return to Wisconsin. New England seemed to fill up an empty place in me, one that I was only peripherally aware of. But, during this time in Boxford, the whole two glorious months of it, I became conscious of a "me" that I had never experienced before, an awkward, shy eleven year old me who grew into a bolder girl, an adventurous girl who wanted to see everything, experience everything and did, from trips to the ocean to eating lobster for the first time.

The Orchard House was our first stop. I had already read *Little Women* many times and my dad knew this would be the place I would want to see first.

I loved Orchard House immediately. There was a comfortable, homey feeling there, blended with hard work and creative energies of different kinds and intensities, the place that held Louisa's secrets and memories, that were part of and included her sisters, the ones that were immortalized in her book *Little Women*. I wanted to know those secrets and also to share mine with Jo. She was real to me, someone Louisa Alcott had made whole and real, a character created out of her longings and joys and fears and the feelings she carried deep inside that made her who she was as a girl and who she would became as a woman. I wanted so much to connect with her, to show her that she and I were alike, one with family and yet apart, to find those things inside her that we could share, that spoke to me and my loneliness.

There was a small building on the grounds near the house. It looked like a small church, or a school, but very rustic, very old and mysterious. I thought of myself inside, what it would be like and what I would do. I imagined listening to conversations about important subjects like history and literature and education, meeting men and women who exchanged brilliant ideas and thoughts, then bidding them good-night at the end of the evening as we went our separate ways, waiting for their return on another evening where we could continue our discussions. Important people with important things to say.

Reluctantly I pulled myself away from the Orchard House and Louisa, as Dad and I headed for the Emerson house, our last stop before we began the return trip to Wisconsin. Dad explained that Ralph Waldo Emerson was a very famous writer and philosopher, who had been a Unitarian minister but left the pulpit to write and lecture here in America and in Europe. He knew the Alcott family very well, especially Bronson, Louisa's father, who was a close friend, a fact that caught my attention immediately.

Everything was different between the two houses. This was a residence that obviously belonged to a family that was financially secure. Inside it was not homey and comfortable as the house where Louisa had lived, even though it was spacious and well furnished. The study was the room that captured my attention. It was where I felt most comfortable, with the old books and the overwhelming feeling that important things were discussed here with colleagues and friends and important words written as well. There was a sense of privacy and well-being, a refuge, where one could center one's self and one's thoughts, away from noise, confusion and distraction. 'This Mr. Emerson must have been a very important man', I thought to myself.

Suddenly we found ourselves in a little room at the top of a staircase. "Henry Thoreau lived here for a few years," Dad said. "This was his room, right here". I peeked inside and felt the world change, for this space was not like the rest of the house. 'He loved it', I thought. 'He gave himself to this little room and felt things and thought things and wrote them down, and the room loved him back because it knew he was grateful to have this space where he could be alone to do his work.'

'Who was he, this Henry Thoreau'? I wondered. I asked Dad, and he said he was another writer like Mr. Emerson, that he wrote a very important book, maybe the most important book written at the time. "People are still reading it today," he said, "more than anyone ever read it in his lifetime. In fact, it's considered a masterpiece, some of the finest writing produced in our American 19th century".

I asked what the book was that Henry Thoreau had written. "It is called *Walden*," Dad said, "and I'll bet when you start high school you'll be reading it in your English class". Henry Thoreau. He was like Louisa then, a writer.

Dad says it is time to get back on the road. We have a long way to go before we reach Wisconsin. As we walk to the car, I pose this question silently: 'What is this place, this Concord? I will never forget you and I will come back someday.' I got into the car to start the long journey back home. 'Why do I love it so much? Why do I feel I belong here?' Someone says from somewhere, "Because it is home".

We stopped at a general store in a little town, just to look around and pick up some snacks. Dad bought me a kerosene lamp, small, but just the right size for me. I was like Jo and I was sure she would have had her very own lamp to read by as she read and wrote her wonderful stories. I had decided I would do the same when I returned home.

Dad said he would build me a tree-house, and I was determined to spend my spare time there writing, thinking deep thoughts and being fiercely independent. The tree-house never got built, but as I grew from the girl who would be Jo, to a woman, the recollection of Jo and the young girl I had been still lived within me. "Home," someone had said a lifetime ago. Concord, my heart responded, it is you.

As I got older, with all the drama and trauma that accompanied me as I tried to get my bearings on my way through the often perilous life of being an adult, pieces of my life reminded me of the chips of colored glass in my grandmother's kaleidoscope that fall into place with the turn of the hand, then completely reconfigure with another turn of the hand that changes the pattern entirely. I decided to return to Concord, many years after my first visit when I was eleven years old. My life had grown more complicated and difficult for me to manage, as I tried to navigate my way through some deep and troubled emotional waters.

As I came within sight of the Colonial Inn and Monument Square, my heart felt it first, an exquisite sensation, as I recalled the word "home" with startling clarity, heard first by my eleven year old self, who believed the word, what it meant, and knew it to be true. 'I have never left', I thought. 'Part of me has always remained here', and I was stunned by the conscious acknowledgement of the truth of it, for it was not a thought, even a memory, but a deep internal knowingness of it as fact. After lunch at the Colonial Inn I planned my first stop, the

Old Manse, Nathaniel and Sophia Hawthorne's first home after they were wed, the house where Ralph Waldo Emerson wrote his monumental work "Nature". Nathaniel and Sophia honeymooned there and began their first years in a fairytale marriage, a marriage that filled in the blank spaces that had left them unfulfilled and incomplete until they met and fell in love.

As I crossed the threshold there was a sensing of them there within the house, the place that still retained the deep love and passion that existed in their relationship.

Every room in the house is full of them, but one room in particular is Nathaniel's alone where he can write the deep dark words that release the Puritan ancestral demons from his soul. Yet even there Sophia can be found, for she is everywhere for him. She has become love for him, and it lives boundaryless, confounding him with its beauty and its purity. 'My dove', he says to her, 'you are the one who brings me peace'. "My love", she replies, "you are the one who gives me strength".

It was hard to leave the Old Manse with the spirits of the two lovers still strong and warm in every room, but I was eager to reacquaint myself with Orchard House. As I pulled into the parking lot I saw it, the little building that had reminded me of a strange little country church and had so enchanted me. I entered the house and felt myself pulled back in time and I remembered being an eleven year old girl, thrilled to be standing in the very house where Louisa Alcott had lived, a sense of familiarity and comfort and recognition of the rooms, the sensing of the family around me. I looked for Jo, but it was Louisa herself that I found instead, where my younger self had found Jo. It made no difference. They were the same, the energy and genius of Louisa May Alcott had created Jo March and so Jo had come to life through her and she has lived in the hearts and minds of millions of readers and has done so for over one hundred fifty years.

Again I felt the desire to curl up in a corner with a book, nestled amidst a pile of pillows to dream, to read, to write, to maybe recover the lost part of myself that had gone missing, to find it again, here in the Alcott family home, but my quest took me somewhere else instead, to the home of Ralph Waldo Emerson.

The house is still beautiful, impressive even today, but when I walk inside I am overwhelmed by the feeling of disappointment and loss, deep, bottomless, a sense of emotional detachment from the man who had lived here and the contraction to protect the heart from someone else, feelings much more intense than the ones I had sensed as a child. Even with servant's gossip, noise from the children at play, it does not matter. The heart of the house is closed, except for the room at the top of the stairs where I had learned from my father that Henry Thoreau had worked in the Emerson household in exchange for room and board. This is where he spent his free time, to write, to dream, to be himself, to be Henry, much as Louisa Alcott had done at Orchard House through her masterful creation of Jo March and her sisters.

There are strong vibrations here, the air alive with creativity and deep thoughts, complex feelings, silent laughter dissolving into tears and tears becoming laughter. I begin to know the Henry Thoreau who lived in this electric space at the top of the stairs.

You work hard and play hard, too", I say aloud. My words were met with silence, but it was silence with an undercurrent of activity, barely discernible, but undeniably there. "You lived here for awhile then went back home then came back here again, dragging your joy and pain back and forth, and your ecstasy and your dreams and your vision. But you carry loss on your shoulders, too, and it is a burden too hard for you to bear. Can you not lay it down in this place? It would be happy, I think, to add your sufferings to what is already here. No? You prefer, then, to carry this load until you defeat it or it puts you in the ground?" There is no answer, and I didn't expect one, but I knew that I had to leave the room at once and the house itself. The energy of Henry Thoreau was too strong, too present, with all of its disappointments and frustrations, despite the occasional contentment and peace he experienced here.

I began my return to Wisconsin the next day, filled with regret that I had to leave Concord, for this is where I knew I belonged, beyond my childhood dreams and expectations. Something happened when I was eleven, an awareness that connected me to this place that I couldn't articulate at the time. I still can't explain it with words like many other things that have happened to me in this life, but I don't feel the need to do so. It is a mystery and I have surrendered myself to it with gratitude.

~ ~ ~

Shortly after my return to Concord I moved to Tucson, Arizona, partly to be in a dry climate due to some health concerns, but also to be near my brother, who had recently moved there. I realized that I needed someplace vast and unknown to me, a place I had never been before like the desert to help me sort out my life which had become confused and uncertain.

I found Tucson to be an alien brown place with too much sun, not enough water, no spring, no colorful autumn, no white radiance of winter that never failed to dazzle me. I didn't know until I didn't have those things how important they were to my sense of well-being. This stripped down bare place, however, was where I did my deepest healing, where there was neither refuge nor escape, as I confronted deep trauma memories buried so efficiently by my unconscious that just a shadow of memory lingered and was easily dismissed where I could tuck it out of mind and out of reach. This avoidance of emotional pain and internal conflict was not what the universe had in mind for me as I soon learned. So with the help of a gifted therapist that my brother recommended, my mind and heart began to clear. Through my own deep work I knew that it was time to go back to Wisconsin. I felt a readiness, a new preparedness, even an obligation to move forward, to begin life anew, with plans and goals to keep me moving toward a new and healthy future.

I returned to a typical end of winter, the last effort of the season to produce cold temperatures and snow reduced to showers rather than blizzards. Winter was beginning to clear the way for spring, softening the trees that were a bit blurry with not-yet-color, the signs that new life was returning.

One evening I was listening to classical music as always, for I was raised on the symphonies of Tchaikovsky, Beethoven, Mozart, Schubert, and all of the great composers of the 17th, 18th, and 19th centuries, including the incomparable piano composers, Liszt and Chopin.

Chopin's etude in E major was playing and I was caught up in a reverie, childhood memories of listening to Chopin as I was tucked into bed for the night. "Chopin died of consumption, too," someone says, a voice that came out of nowhere. After a moment I turned my attention once again to the music, bewildered, listening for more, but there was nothing.

A few days later I received my usual bargain book catalog in the mail that kept me well supplied with books that I could afford. Looking through it I came across the biography section, and as I scanned the pages I came across a title that looked interesting, **The Thoreau You Don't Know**. It sounded like the perfect book for me. I *did* want to know more about this man. I still remembered his little room at the Emerson home in Concord that had distressed me so much, the feeling of those conflicted energies of the man that had lived there while working for his room and board. I recalled conversations with my father long ago that Henry Thoreau had lived in Concord, Massachusetts all of his life, he knew the Alcott and the Emerson families very well and had a cordial relationship with Nathaniel Hawthorne. Of course I wanted to know more about him and this was the perfect opportunity to do so.

In the catalog, the cover of the book was represented by a cartoon-y looking face drawn with simple black lines on a white background. One eye is open, very green, the other closed in an audacious wink. 'How sassy,' I think. 'Very amusing. A compelling way to sell a book.' There is so much to tell, that face says to me. So much to know.

Curious and a bit expectant about something, though I'm not quite sure about what it is that I'm expecting, I take the bait and buy the book, completely up for the challenge I imagine I see in that face. I read it from cover to cover when I received it, hating to put it down, and when I finished the book I looked again at the face on the cover. Read more, I heard. There is more that you need to know. Did I know where those words came from and who said them? Yes. I knew where those words came from and who said them, and I felt the final piece of healing fall into place, like a missing piece of a puzzle, the one piece that had been missing, even with all the healing work I had done when I lived in Arizona three years earlier. Now it was finally complete.

So my journey began, or should I say it continued, for in fact it began when I was eleven years old with my dad, being tourists like thousands of other people, going to the Orchard House and the Bush, the home of RalphWaldo Emerson and his family. It was there in Concord, Massachusetts that I received my first clues, intimations of something or about someone that I was too young to understand, but everything became clearer when I returned years later as an adult, though the specifics of what I was feeling still continued to elude me.

This was the first book I read about Henry Thoreau, and the life that I had known, or thought I knew, changed irrevocably.

What happened to me after reading that book broke me open, emotionally, psychologically. All of the things that had been lost to me, in both conscious and unconscious memory, the feeling that something was missing, was lost or gone, were restored.

The Thoreau That You Don't Know brought it all back. It was the catalyst that brought me to the edge of an awareness that had eluded me all of my life. What began in Concord when I was a young girl, those sensings, deepened, with the certainty of why I felt such a strong connection to that small New England village. And Henry David Thoreau was the key.

I had fallen in love with him. I love him. And how did I account for this, loving a man I had never met who lived in the nineteenth century, born in 1817, a man that had been relatively unknown to me but for one or two common facts, that he wrote a book called **Walden** and he lived in the woods for a couple of years?

This was the extent of my knowledge of Henry Thoreau, until I read the book that changed my life. This is the 21st century, two hundred years after he was born. It is true, I said to myself. When I was in the Emerson house and in Henry's room, I felt him, with all of the nuances and highs and lows of that complex nature that made him who he was while he was alive. But that was his *energy*.

As I continue reflecting on what I have read in what I refer to as "The Book", reliving memories from my two trips to Concord, both as a child and an adult, and the sense impressions that I was left with both times it has become clear. It is Ellen Sewall that I am feeling within me, the Ellen that Henry loved in Concord, Massachusetts, when he was a young man of twenty-two and she a girl of seventeen, the girl Robert Sullivan writes about in his book, **The Thoreau You Don't Know**.

Ellen was the only woman Henry proposed to and when her parents refused to let her marry him, because he was not considered a suitable match, the relationship came to an unhappy end. Henry remained single for the rest of his life.

This is how I experience Henry, through reflection and the memory of sensing him in Concord, not just the public persona that he presented to the world in which he lived and how he was perceived by his neighbors and friends, but in a deeply personal way, as a lover, as a woman who wanted to be his wife. That is how and why I know that I love him. For I began to realize that I was Ellen Sewall in that lifetime and all of who I was then, all of who Henry had been to me, and all I had been to him came back to me into my present day consciousness as a life I had once lived as another woman almost two hundred years ago.

I know about past or former lifetimes. It is not a new concept to me, but what I didn't know was how much in the present a former life can feel, at least this is my experience as I felt the awareness of my being Ellen Sewall coming back to my conscious memory.

But there is more to it than that. I could have just responded to everything that I was experiencing as an interesting phenomenon, that I was experiencing the recall of a former life, the love of Henry Thoreau and the man whom I had loved and wanted to marry. And I could have gotten on with my life without much more thought about it than that, but something was guiding me forward to a fuller and deeper response. I realized that I needed to learn more about Henry, and to do that I needed to read everything that had ever been written about him.

I began with Walter Harding's *The Days of Henry Thoreau*, next *A Life of the Mind,* by Robert Richardson, book after book about Henry and everything he wrote as well, his two books *A Week on the Concord and Merrimack River* and *Walden,* his essays and journals and I spent days, weeks, months reading.

I believe that the conclusion that I had reached months earlier was true, that I *did* have a former life as Henry Thoreau's love, Ellen Sewall and that the love we felt for each other, that began in 19th century Concord, Massachusetts never died with our physical deaths.

I live in two realities now. My physical world here, which is connected to the world where Henry lives, the spiritual realm, and both of us are connected to the world where we had met and fallen in love, in nineteenth century Concord; the trail that led me back to him begins there.

I am going to do something unusual here and in a few other places throughout this book. I have asked Henry to speak in his own words. Much has happened since I rediscovered the connection between Henry and myself and it will become clearer to you as you continue reading this narrative. This is how it is done: Because I am clairaudient, which, as I explained earlier, is the ability to hear with "spirit ears", Henry and I can communicate with each other. We speak across worlds, from his to mine, mine to his, and I can hear him and, of course, as a spirit soul he can hear me. I asked him to relate in *his* words about Ellen and the love they felt for each other. I have written down what he said to me, and I am sharing it with you here.

~ ~ ~

The love between Ellen Sewall and myself, that is the love that I can speak to personally. My intention is to explain the differences and similarities that exist in our love that began in Concord, Massachusetts and our love now because you may have questions. Perhaps I can answer them here.

I must give some background to our story, part of which you might already know, those of you who have read about Ellen and me. When we met in Concord we were very young and all that we knew of love was what we felt for our parents, siblings and friends. Our feelings for each other did not blossom immediately, for Ellen was but a child still and no lasting impression of each other was felt by either one of us.

Upon renewing our acquaintance when she came to visit relatives, particularly her brother and other family members who were lodging with us in my family's boarding house, we were both a few years older and thus susceptible to those first early stirrings of the heart that foretell the possibility of incredible things to come.

I was the first to succumb. And I was pulled, neither gently nor carefully, by the violence of an impact so sudden that I felt as if I had been taken by a tidal wave down to the depths of my heart, never to recover or to return to the shore of my previous existence, nor did I want to. I had discovered the wonder and joy of my first love, and my heart opened with the truth of that fact. I surrendered to it utterly.

My darling surrendered as well in her own way in her own time, a flooding of her being as she described it to me, with soft light that reflected my very self back to her, lodging forever in her heart. This love, though so different in its beginnings from mine, presented itself as it did for me, fixed, with no other purpose but to remain steadfast and strong. This was the love that we felt, with and without words, for our time alone was rare. It lived in our deep silences where a mere touch of the hand or a stolen glance was as powerful to us as the sharing of a marriage bed.

It was our misfortune that Ellen's mother and father considered me an unsuitable match for their daughter, unable to secure her happiness. Both were immovable in their opposition to me and so Ellen and I were parted, all of our future plans in tatters. We moved on to live our lives in different ways, sometimes with satisfaction, even joy, but with unresolved longings for each other that could not be replaced by anyone or anything.

Here is the essential question that some of you may have: Is the love we feel for each other now different than it was then, when we were in love in a different lifetime? I say it is the same, with this explanation: It is the same love as it was in the beginning, the same first love that we felt in Concord, the essence of it, the genesis of it, if you will. But it is now exalted and purified, because it has been transformed. It is free from the limitations that color every physical relationship, however unintentionally. Ellen and I were no different in that regard. We loved as deeply as any two people can, but the love we share now is more rare and fine because it is untainted by human imperfection, a burden most of us share or have shared before we move to a different realm after death.

Would I have preferred to love her then the way I do now? No. I would not change one moment of those yearnings that lived in my embodied heart. They were and still are precious to recall. The depth of our commitment to each other and our will to love beyond death has led us here to this time where we are reunited and so we say we are together now "beyond the beyond the beyond." And so it is, ever and anon, my love, ever and anon.

I have offered these words to all who love as we did, to all who are committed to love beyond death as we were and are, with hopes that your prayers will be answered, your dreams of eternal life together fulfilled. May it be so for you as it has been for my love and me. -- Henry Thoreau

~ ~ ~

It is May 14, 2013.

"My love, you bring me joy." As these words penetrate my consciousness I am almost overcome with shock. I quiet myself, straining to hear more, but there is nothing. It is Henry, unbelievably it is Henry speaking to me. The following day there is this: "You bring me joy. Don't ever leave me." It was Henry Thoreau, recognizing me as the woman who had been Ellen Sewall, just as I had known it for the previous two months. During that time, those two months that I read and read about Henry, I felt something I had never experienced before: a deep sense of personal fulfillment, a joy, the kind of feeling one has when finally reunited with the one beloved, the eternal, soul connected beloved.

After the first words from Henry on May 14th and 15th, as unexpected and stunning as they were, we had frequent conversations throughout the day and into the night. We easily found the words again that neither of us had spoken to each for over 150 years. There was not a strange or awkward moment, no feeling of distance separating us, for in fact there was *not*. There are no physical walls, no barriers between worlds. We communicated effortlessly as if we were speaking to each other on the telephone. For two weeks I kept a record of everything. I had a notebook with me at all times so that I didn't miss a word of what we said to each other, but it soon became obvious that it was impossible to continue to keep a written account of our conversations.

~ ~ ~

This is a story that is hard for me to speak of, but it has a place here so it must be told. It is my story, it could be yours someday or something very like it. But this is mine and it belongs here as part of this narrative as it unfolds.

When Ellen lay dying, many years after my own passing, I went to her to bring her home with me to my world, and we lived here which became our home, reunited and filled with the joy of it. Too soon she was taken from me, a soul contract that she needed to fulfill in a new physical life far away from me in the temporal world again. She assumed a new role with a different identity, a new physical form and I watched her, felt every beat of her heart, every breath she took. She was lost to me, but I waited for her to return, knowing her life would be short. For she would die as a young girl and before long in physical time she returned and once again we were together.

Our lives were rich and full again with the promise of our eternal life together. What we had forgotten in our joy of being together again was that there was yet another separation to come, and of course it came too soon. This time it would be many years in physical time, for she would stay in the temporal world well into her middle years and beyond, with many trials to endure and much pain to overcome. What I saw, what I felt, the challenges she had to experience, filled me with a sense of dread and despair. I could not help her or reach her. Again I was forgotten as she lived another life in the physical world.

I could not dispel that sense of dread and despair, though I tried desperately to calm myself. I could no longer bear the pain of her being gone from me, for I was convinced that she would come back to me greatly changed. The Elders here who tend to us -- for yes, we still need help occasionally and guidance even here -- counseled me with words from their wise, ancient minds and kind hearts. They saw me turn from them, even though they assured me that this was the last separation we would ever have to endure. I heard nothing. My heart had gone cold within me and no longer sustained me. She will return, yes, I thought, but will she love me still? Will she want to love me after what she will have lived through in her last physical life, with abuse and suffering at the hands of men? Will she turn from me, preferring to be alone, to live an eternal life apart from me?

I willed myself to go to what is called the Dark Place, consciously and with intention, because I had no answers to my agonizing questions. This Dark Place is not what those of the Christian faith called Hell. It is worse. Intention puts you there due to one's ignorance and refusal to commit to the indwelling divine principle that calls eternally for life and love. There is no release once you are there, for there is not enough of your own energy to bring you back.

The energy of one's soul body is diminished to the point of almost being extinguished. And so one lingers, neither dead nor alive, and neither love nor light, except the dimmest flicker remains, the last remnant of the light that barely sustains life or thought or feeling. All desire is gone, all sense of life, even the memory of what life is, except the shadow of that memory which remains to torment what is left of the soul. And you are lost forever there. This is what I had decided to do to myself, where I had decided to go, for life without my love was no life at all, and I had convinced myself that it would be so. I had become faithless and reckless, a dangerous combination for an arrogant individual such as myself.

My decision was made and I would not be persuaded to change my mind, for free choice, free will reigns supreme here as it does on earth. The terrors of the Dark Place were insignificant compared to the possibility that I would never see love for me in my beloved's eyes again.

I see that earlier in this memoir my love spoke about her journey to Tucson, Arizona, but what she didn't say is what I'm telling you now. She was being made ready to find me again, for without her own accelerated healing she would not have been able to find me or recognize me while she was still embodied. She had to be made as clear, as pure as possible to be able to feel the love, recognize the heart link that connected us and to increase her own vibrational level.

Without these changes she would be unable to find me until she died, and that was determined not to be an option by the Elders who were watching over us both, due to my imminent decision to leave my soul life behind in the Dark Place. They told me that my love would buy a book and that she would remember herself as Ellen again from a previous existence, who would recall loving me and being loved where it all began for us in Concord, Massachusetts.

The grace I was granted to forestall my irresponsible actions was the information given to me by the Elders about my beloved and the joy she felt upon remembering me and our love. Despair turned to hope, along with feelings of shame for my cowardice and lack of faith, but all who are here can see their weaknesses and be inspired by the bright beings who help us to make better choices as our eternal lives here continue to unfold. My love and I continue our journey together, though she is in one world and I in another, but she will have more to say about it. It is for her to do so. -- Henry Thoreau

On May 18, 2013, 9:50 pm. Henry says, "You are my soul wife. My love, you are my one true wife." I call out to him, "Beloved, say it again, that I am your soul wife." This is the first time Henry has ever called me his wife. I ask him to explain, and he says that Elder beings in the world where he lives witnessed our vows and the exchange of rings that Henry made from the light that surrounds him and my aura colors, signifying an eternal pledge that has woven our souls, each to each, eternally. We will never have to part again.

I spoke these words to my wife, asking if she would record them. Would that I could have written them myself in my life that has passed, these painful recollections that I will now relate. They belong here, nevertheless, in her narrative, a place of truth-telling, confession perchance, a way to prove myself more worthy of her and her love. All may read these words as well and credit as true and reasonable the comments my friends and acquaintances who knew me made about my conduct. They could not have felt worse about me then I did about myself at the time.

My wife married me, knowing that I carried within me still, the seeds of rage and agony that fed one another, first one in ascendance, then the other and worse feelings as well. For many reasons I felt abandoned and alone. Even the cherished and deepest affections that I found in nature was no longer my greatest comfort and solace.

I remained unconsoled for the most part, nursing grievances and deliberately misunderstanding lessons being presented to me from a kind and benevolent universe. I cringe even now to reflect upon my unworthy thoughts and behavior. There was no heart within me to respond to kindness from others and the joy of being alive, despite what you may read about me from others who know me not, because they were not there. They have not now, nor had not then, any way of knowing what was in my poor closed heart or what I thought. Some of my own words betray me as false and a liar. Did I present myself well in company when called upon to socialize or when I felt it was in my best interest to do so, being too often alone with grievous thoughts? Sometimes yes, sometimes no. Mr. Emerson will attest to the fact that the answer was "no" much of the time.

All of this and more I brought to the world where I live now, conflicted as I was, unrepentant and in unimaginable pain. With the loss of John, my brother, I should have had Ellen to help me bear the loss, but she was taken as well, for we could not marry. I was an unsuitable match, according to her parents, and I lost her to someone else.

It is enough to say that my wife found me again, as she has explained to you. It was she who saved me when she came to my world for the first time and found me. It was she who held me as I raged and wept, as I grieved anew for John who died in my arms. I believed his loss would surely kill me. I grieved also for the loss of her, feelings that still held me in their grip even here, until with my wife's love for me and compassion for my suffering, their hold on me was finally loosened, and I was able to let them go.

I am reunited with John, for he held sacred space for me here until I could join him and with Ellen, my soul wife at last, the one who would finally help shape my life here and give it greater depth and purpose. I can now do for her and be for her all that she asks of me and so much more. Ellery Channing is here as well, for he is my closest friend, and I would not change him, as contrary and unpredictable as he is, for any man I have ever known. All is well now and I am content, for I am complete. -- Henry Thoreau

~ ~ ~

I want to say a few words about Ellery Channing, Henry's best friend and walking companion. I see now, by my marriage to Henry, something I didn't know before, how grief in the physical world can live on in the hearts and minds of souls, even into their new lifetimes after death. Henry's brother John died of lockjaw in his arms, and it changed him, ending his familiar world and remaking it into something unrecognizable. Ellery Channing, who was his friend, found a way into his wounded heart by hearing what it said and speaking to it, despite Henry's impenetrable silences, which is where he so desperately needed to be heard.

Ellery was the one friend Henry loved despite marked differences in their characters and personalities, for they also had much in common. What Henry got from Ellery was an abiding friendship with large doses of irreverence, coarse humor, even though he found it intolerable at times and a lack of sentimentality, which suited Henry perfectly. What Henry gave in return was tolerance for Ellery's occasional unpardonable conduct, empathy for Ellery's sensitive poetic nature, loyalty and an intuitive sensing of what emotional and psychological shadows plagued this troubled man. In some ways they were mirrors reflecting one another's psyches, both the light sides and the dark, that made them uniquely compatible. Excursions and sauntering forged the links that bound them together, close enough to be comfortable and supportive when needed, yet with enough distance between them to be able to maintain their independence from one another.

What did I see when I looked at Henry? What did he look like through my clairvoyant eyes? My first impression was that he was young, twenty or twenty-one years old perhaps, short hair, very thick with a slight wave, falling below his ears, a light to medium brown color, and some strains of red mixed throughout. He is a bit below medium height, thin and wiry, but looks strong and well grounded. It is his face that is so arresting. His eyes are large in his lean face, blue and grey so that the exact color is imprecise. His nose is prominent, but suits the rest of his face, bringing into balance his eyes and sensitive, expressive mouth.

This is how I saw Henry in the early days and weeks of our marriage. As the weeks went by I was surprised to notice a change in his appearance. He was no longer the young man that I had first seen, but was now significantly older, the image of the Maxham daguerreotype that appears in many places on the walls of my apartment and is the most common representation of Henry, seen in many of the books written about him.

This was the man that I see now and always will, for he will not change again. I recognize the features of that young man, the way he looked when I fell in love with him, but I see now the struggles that he endured in his short life, written in his careworn face, etched there and weathered from the days and nights of rambles and saunters that helped bring some measure of peace and sanity to his physical existence.

I see wrinkles at the corners of his eyes and a Galway beard and longer hair that needs tending. Where he lives now he will receive no censure for his personal appearance. I see suffering that still lingers in his eyes from a lifetime in Concord with disappointments and the pain of remembered grief, the occasional feelings of the futility of his life where his voice was not heard, whether written or spoken. I see this, but also I see love, deep love for me and the joy that our marriage has brought him, that has filled the empty unfulfilled places in his life, as they have filled mine.

I didn't understand the change I noticed in his appearance, so I asked him about it. He explained how important it was, *imperative* to appear to me as I had known him in Concord when I was Ellen, as opposed to seeing him as a man much changed. Henry was right. Seeing him the way I remembered him when I was Ellen was an important way to transition from then to now and increased my comfort level and sense of wellbeing, as I began the incredible journey of being Henry David's wife.

He dresses simply and with good sense as he did in Concord. No frock coat ever, but this instead: Two collarless shirts, one pale blue with a muted white stripe, the other a soft cream color; heavy denim pants, but grey not blue, a pair of steel-toed boots for heavy activity and inclement weather and a softer pair of boots that lace up, both pairs that come over his ankles. His hat is now dark grey with a wide brim. In winter he has a heavy blue wool jacket, but I have never seen him with gloves or a scarf. In the spring and summer, no coat but the hat remains. It is his favorite piece of apparel, which he wears regardless of the weather, rain or shine.

The early days of our marriage were hopefully what most newlyweds share, yet with significant differences, of course. This was and is a soul marriage, and yet we experience many of the things that physical partners do. My husband had been celibate when he lived in the physical world, but souls can and do make love.

I will protect our privacy by saying nothing more, except to explain that loving Henry is an exchange of energy rather, of course, than an act of love with physical bodies. It is the merging of our souls that blend and absorb one another, significantly more intense and nuanced than embodied physical love, however that inexpressible bliss that I felt with Henry was also accompanied by the intense shift for me of having to adjust to being a soul wife while still embodied in this lifetime. Henry, in turn, had to grapple with the reality of becoming a husband for the first time and as a soul husband. Those were our days as newlyweds and we have both learned, in truth are still learning how to accommodate each other in this unusual marriage, for I still have an embodied life. The time we spend together is limited to the nighttime hours for the reason that I am still embodied, an agreement that was made with the Elders in Henry's world who witnessed our marriage. Those are the limitations they have imposed upon us, and so it will be until I am no longer a part of this physical world, when I will then be able to join Henry permanently.

For the first few months of my new marriage I would often experience moments of terror upon waking in the morning. It was the realization that I was no longer with my husband. I had been with Henry in his world throughout the night, returning here to reenter my embodied self and this physical world in the early hours of the morning. The adjustment of leaving his world and coming back to mine was a shock to my system. The trauma was extreme on those occasions, and I would cry out for him, believing that he was gone forever, for I could no longer feel him as my physical body was trying to readjust itself to this world.

Though these terrible fears returned occasionally, I was reassured and comforted by my new husband, imploring me to look into his eyes as he spoke, so that I would know, not only by the sound of his voice, but by the love that I would see there that he was with me, that he would never leave me, that my fears were a part of the adjustment that I would have to make every morning, when I returned to the physical world. Our soul marriage was, however, eternal and the connection would never be broken from his world to mine. We have proven that love does not recognize boundaries, barriers, walls, different worlds, different centuries. When hearts are engaged and the desire and will to stay connected is declared not even death can separate two souls.

~ ~ ~

This is Henry's world that he created, where he lives now and also where I go to be with him every night: There is the pond, identical to his beloved Walden, forests so dense he can get lost in them, a rural village like Concord, the way it was when he was growing up without the encroaching threat of industrialization, hills, valleys, cliffs where he can sit and gaze at the beautiful landscape below, and of course, swamps and wildlife, and every kind of bird he can remember from his life and some that he had never seen before as well.

Our house is on a rise overlooking the pond, a house that Henry and his brother John built after we married. It is similar to the house he lived in at Walden Pond in Concord, but a bit larger to accommodate a wife, though without luxuries. For I share his philosophy about living a simple life.

His green desk is there in front of the window in our sitting room where he spends time writing, and he stays home writing or reading, mostly reading now, until he leaves to meet John for a long saunter or waits for John to come to him, when they both set off like the boys they still are for the adventure of the day. This is my description, but for a more complete picture and understanding of how it all came about I have asked Henry to explain it in his words, how this world where he lives was created.

    I have been asked by my wife to clarify her remarks about my world, how I have made it my own, apparently without benefit of materials to create a house, for instance, or how, indeed, rivers, hills, woods and the like appear in this wonderful place that I call home.
    I confess that I was at a loss when I arrived here, knowing nothing, expecting I knew not what, but in short order I was given into the hands of gentle, loving beings who tended to me with great care, who asked me in the most loving supportive ways what I required to make my life here peaceful and congenial after losing my temporal home. I answered forthwith, with no hesitation, for I recognized the grace and love with which questions were put to me.
    I said that I required what I had left behind, my village of Concord, but more. For my life here, the depth and quality depended upon it. "I need trees", I said. "I need all living things around me, animals, birds, water, yes, water, which to me, has always been alive. My world here will be insupportable without these comforts to ease my way here. I need all of the wondrous things that I found in Nature while I lived in the physical world.
    "Can it be?" I asked. "May I have the very things here that I had there, all the things that brought me joy when I sought refreshment in solitude?"
    The simple answer came to me in one blessed word, "Yes." It is a matter of will, I was told, when I asked for more clarity. "If you *will* it, if you want it with pure intention, you will create it in what is called 'thought form.' Your world here will be as specific and complete as you require it to be, with no change or interference from any other being here. Wish for it, think it, believe it, it will manifest here for you. And if you wish to change any aspect of your original idea or plan, that will happen as well. Your world is here now, made

for your particular requirements, including any companions with whom you choose to share your life, with their consent, of course.

I made my world then, as my wife has described it to you, with my brother John who waited for me to come to him and Ellery Channing, my friend and companion who was eager to join us when his time came to leave the physical world.

I will say another word to dispel any confusion about the physical nature of, for example, the building of my house. My wife has already said that John and I built a new house to accommodate the two of us after we were married, and so we did. My world, the one that I "ordered," that I willed into being, is physical. There is nothing here that I cannot touch, smell, hear, appreciate with all of my senses. The difference is simply that all of my senses are magnified to a high degree, as are my physical surroundings, though they look like what I enjoyed while I lived in Concord. My entire natural world is here, but because my senses are much more acute, so my environment is more highly developed and attuned to me. Colors are brighter, birds sing with more clarity and sweetness, trees are taller and more broad in thicker forests.

This is what I have made here, the world which I inhabit, but it is complete only because I have the companionship of my brother John, my friend Ellery Channing and my wife, when she can be here to share time with me in the nighttime hours. -- Henry Thoreau

~ ~ ~

"It seemed as if the breezes brought him.
"It seemed as if the sparrows taught him.

Ralph Waldo Emerson

I feel I should speak here about my last illness, not that it is important in and of itself, but so that I can state the facts, which are so important, there being some misconceptions about that time that must be set right.

I will speak about what I was thinking, if I can recall and how I felt. It matters not to me, of course, for I am beyond all of it. What I say perhaps is relevant to those who have a curiosity about it, but if not, then what I say can easily be forgotten.

I recall saying that I leave the world without regret or something like it. Of course that was not true. I regretted much, but I was in the habit of speaking in such a way to guard against too much sympathy, too much concern on my behalf, and also not to alarm my mother and sister Sophia, who were already suffering from the loss of John, Helen and father.

My deepest regret -- I will use that inadequate word 'regret' -- is that I would be losing the woods, rivers, fields where I sauntered, hills, swamps, all of which were more than my second home. They were what made many of the authentic parts of me, as if we were one, and I believe that we were. I found my voice there, to speak thoughts and ideas that were not popular in the village and often not with my friends. But I was shaped and encouraged to be what I was by these wonderful places, where I spent so much of my time. They were home to the bright beings, who helped give voice to many of the things that were most important to me, that taught me the right way to live, that knew my heart.

I had too much pride to reveal the despair I felt, regarding the decline in my health, a grievous fault of which I was aware. I have been relieved of the burden of carrying that pride into my new life. It has no place here. My brother John and Ellen were gone from me, the two people I loved best in the world, the only ones who would have been able to bring me a measure of peace and solace to ease my fear and accept the inevitable.

I wanted to die well when the time came, using John as an example. My passing from life was said to be easy and peaceful. It was not easy, it was not peaceful, though I used all of my strength to make it appear so to spare my mother and sister. I would not let myself dwell on thoughts of Ellen, but they came unbidden to me. When I heard her name spoken -- perhaps it was Sophia who spoke of her -- I could not refrain from saying: "I have always loved her." The wind and water carried the sound of her name, too, and the trees and flowers, *everything* in my world wherever I went knew how much I loved her.

There is no ending to what has been, there is no beginning to what will be. My death was simply a continuing, rather, of love and life. Love that was found there in the physical world where I lived for a time and here as well, eternity made manifest here in that life that I once had, beyond waking and sleeping dreams. Thus it is that my joy is no imaginary thing but real. For it lives in my life here and in the love that Ellen and I share, the emptying of ourselves into each other and filling each other again, to begin again each day that way, *beyond the beyond the beyond.*

I am going to speak now in my own words to add to what Henry has said about his last days, for those of you who have not read what has already been recorded by friends and family who were there with him. Henry never realized what a vital part of the Concord community he had been or how deeply he was loved.

It is spring in Concord, Massachusetts, early May, 1862. A man is in the parlor of the house where he has lived for twelve years. His bedroom is in the attic, the room that holds his books, his papers, the most precious things that he has collected in his short lifetime. For he is not quite forty-five years old.

He can't spend time there anymore, for he is too weak to go up and down the stairs. The parlor has become his bedroom, his sitting room and his study. He continues to write until he is too weak to hold a pen. So his sister Sophia takes on the task of recording his spoken words, even though he can barely speak above a whisper. He is able to sit, for at times it is easier for him to breathe when he is not reclining. Friends who love him come to call and his mother and sister tend to him, trying to keep him comfortable and as cool as possible. For it is a warm spring and consumption has him in the grip of fever during the day and night sweats when he tries and fails to fall asleep.

Sophia places the furniture just so at his request, with objects near that will cast shadows on the walls of the room as the light begins to fade, in order to keep him distracted from the pain that constantly threatens to overwhelm him.

Amos Bronson Alcott comes, one of many of Henry's friends who wish to pay their respects. He steps quietly into the parlor and beholding the pale and wasted face approaches the makeshift bed. As he beholds his dying friend he leans over and kisses his forehead. Hands are briefly clasped, a whisper of thanks and good-by. Henry hears a woman's name that he has carried in his heart for over twenty years . He thinks of her now and says to his sister, "I have always loved her." He will carry her in his heart when he dies, holding her close with his very last thought and breath.

These are my thoughts, based on what I have read of Henry's last days. They may sound melodramatic, but what I have read about his dying time was just so, with no melodrama, just the facts of it were clear enough. His premature loss was tragic, and his loss was keenly felt, not by just his family and friends, but by the Concord community as well, who too late, realized what an irreplaceable treasure he was.

As an adult I have spent my life searching for answers to questions that I asked, but the answers only pointed to a direction which could neither fulfill nor satisfy me. Something was there, just beyond reach, everything the word symbols pointed to, and everything inside of me yearned to recall what that "everything" was.

Henry Thoreau was the one to whom the word symbols were pointing, with his beingness that I finally came to recognize, that saturated every thought, every feeling, every word that he wrote. And, as I read his words, I remembered being Ellen Sewall and I felt her, but I also felt myself being Henry and all of the universe, mystery upon mystery expanding, re-creating and enlarging the concept of life itself, beyond the parameters of human consciousness.

Again, and I can't overemphasize it enough, it is a mystery, *the* mystery of life, of love, that can cross time from one century to another. For there is nothing to separate one beloved from another, if they choose to love each other, even after death and across time and space.

There are physical places on this planet that are magic, not magical, which is a weak adjective, but *magic,* a word that has deep roots in the divine mysteries, attributed, perhaps to energy lines, like the microcosm of longitude and latitude lines of the earth. It could be that, or perhaps it has to do with metaphysical time that is still as alive now in Concord as it was almost two hundred years ago.

I speak of the time when a group of individuals lived in that small New England village in the mid 19th century. Each felt connected to the other, despite age differences, diverse opinions and personalities that often clashed, as each man sought to express his unique thoughts and ideas that birthed the *new* thought, the challenge of a new kind of idealism and self-culture called Transcendentalism.

New ideas were exchanged, old perceptions challenged, some of those ideas finding fertile ground in the minds and hearts of those most adventurous seekers. Wisdom of the mind, but also of the heart, a call that one man heard and was determined to integrate, two parts becoming one, and he lived his life from the integrity of that new paradigm. Henry David Thoreau was his name.

Concord is not the only place in the world like this, but it is *my* place, where I felt that magic for the first time as an eleven year old girl, magic that is part of the ponds, the trees, the grasses, flowers, even within the very structures of the old buildings themselves, the stones, bricks, mortar, wood that were shaped by men into houses and shops and farms that held the energy of the place.

The strands of 19th century Concord are woven within those of the 20th and 21st centuries. They are the very fabric of the community, made up of thoughts, which became words, which became actions. Henry lived there all of his life and gave all of himself to it, this Concord, this beloved place he called home. He is the very poem he said he could write, the human and divine part of the heart, blood, bone and sinew of the village. He is still there in so many ways, in so many places and always will be for those who believe. Concord, Massachusetts and Henry can never be separated completely. It is still Henry's home in this world and always will be, for he would have it so.

I hope that I have brought this man to life for you, this wonder of a man who has become my husband. That is miracle enough, and the challenge for me as the author of this offering was to make Henry live through my words and his as well. He can be outspoken still, though his temperament has softened to the point that some of his old friends would find his chastened spirit quite unlike the Henry they knew in life.

This is the man *I* know, the quieter, more reflective man. There are no political battles to fight; no acres of woodland being decimated for the building of houses or barns, or to use as fuel for fireplaces or stoves; no misunderstandings with friends; no heartbreak over lost love or loved ones. I see and love a different Henry, and I have tried to bring him to life for you so that you can know him, too.

Henry Thoreau, the man, still lives in Henry Thoreau, the soul. I would know him anywhere, for he is forever shaped by that identity, the man that I fell in love with in Concord, Massachusetts almost two hundred years ago.

I live and love in two worlds now and I shall until Henry comes to bring me home, where we will live together always in our house by our own Walden, walking with John and Ellery.

Through this narrative I hope that you have been able to find Henry again in a new, more living way, seeing him with as unique a perspective as I come to behold him, as soul-being and also as the man most recognizable to those who have read what he has written and what has been written about him. Henry David Thoreau is there, waiting to be rediscovered. There is just more of him, for he is complete now, always Henry, ever and anon.

Claire Russell

POSTSCRIPT

I met Stuart Weeks, founder of The Center for American Studies at Concord, at the Thoreau Society Gathering in 2017. I spent some hours talking to him, telling him the story that you have read in these pages, something that I had revealed to only two of my closest friends. What I said to him was controversial, perhaps even outrageous and unbelievable to some, but he believed me and encouraged me to write what I had told him and share my words with those who cared to read my story, who could perhaps see it as part of their own experience.

Stuart has written the word to the Reader and the postscript that follows. He has a deep love and reverence for Henry Thoreau, and so it is right that Stuart is represented here by his words, a welcome addition to my testament that has been written for you.

Claire Russell

~ ~ ~

Thoreau Bicentennial Presentation, July 16, 2017

The Thoreau We Do Not Yet Know

Stuart-Sinclair Weeks, Founder,
The Center for American Studies at Concord

> *People say today: He is not a true scientist who does not determine observation and experiment quite logically; who does not pass from thought to thought in strict conformity with the correct methods that have evolved. If he does not do this, he is no genuine thinker. But, my dear friends, what if reality happens to be an artist and scorns our elaborate, dialectical and experimental methods? What if nature herself works according to artistic impulses? If it were so, human science, according to nature, would have to become artistic, for otherwise there would be no possibility of understanding nature.* *

I would like to begin, friends, with thanks, thanks to our hosts, "brothers" here in Concord's Masonic Lodge — founded by a gentleman whose name is coupled with a memorable verse, Paul

Revere himself. If my recollection serves me rightly, we are also, and appropriately, gathered in what in days past was Henry David's old school house.

I extend my thanks to all the speakers at this bounteous bicentennial celebration of Concord's native son, near and dear to all our hearts. Thanks, in particular, to those with whom I had the occasion to share words over these days of celebration.

My thoughts go to Jay (Amaran), who made the journey from India, where he has introduced Henry David as the Guiding Spirit of the "Earth Scouts"; Sile (Post), whose book *The Road to Walden North* has brought Henry David alive to many an otherwise *non*-transcendentalist student; Jacob (Hundt), whose fledgling Thoreau College in Viroqua, Wisconsin is seeking to do just that for, and with, the up and coming generation; John (Bullard), whose appreciation for Concord's Native Son is (as noted in the "Word to the Reader") inspired by the 12 Step path and fellowships; Dr. James (Mathews), a Gandhian/Thoreavian, as we'll see; and Connie (Baxter Marlow), who, as we speak, is offering a presentation in the room below us on: "Spiritual Disobedience, Spiritual Activism & Higher Laws." Thank you for lifting our vision, Connie. May we never lose such laws out of sight. My thoughts go to these kindred spirits, among others.

Thank you, Mike (Frederick), Executive Director of the Thoreau Society, and your fellow trustees for envisioning and bringing to life this memorable gathering, dotting the innumerable i's and crossing the immeasurable t's. As this bicentennial celebration draws toward its conclusion has it been the gathering, might I ask, that you envisioned?

I, my self, have attended these celebrations of the Thoreau Society for nearly four decades. Upon reflection, there has been a quality to this annual meeting that has distinguished it for me, a quality I would speak of as a certain "selflessness." It has been clear that the words shared have come not — with ALL respects due — from "academics" alone, "critical thinkers," but from those of a less scholarly bent no less, whose love for Henry David is deep and abiding. As I trust you can imagine, Henry David takes his hat off, in particular, to the latter.

In terms of setting the tone for this offering of mine, I return to Wen (Stephenson's) opening keynote address. Wen you shared passages from Henry David's essay *Civil Disobedience* and then went on to take our dear president, Donald John Trump, to task — along with certain members of his cabinet, who, you noted, have not exhibited a particular regard for our environment, earth, our very foundation.

Forthright you were, Wen, in your concern not only about mass extinction, but with respect to the small window you behold that we're still granted, in order to avert the unfolding crisis. This is not scare-mongering, you noted, but facts. "Issues are political, which is to say they are moral." Which, might one add, Wen, is to say that they are spiritual — if we could give compelling meaning to that word?

Wen spoke of crimes against the earth and humanity and was unabashed — indeed Thoreauvian — in stating that "a radical situation demands a radical response" — one that gets to the *radicalis* (in Latin), to the very *root* of the problem before us. "That is, we need to get serious, ever more so. We need a social and political movement, such as those that have transformed history in the past. We need to face the facts; find out what we are made of and act. To lay everything on the line: our regulations, careers.... bodies, maybe even our lives. Let your light be a counter friction to stop the machine," you noted, invoking HDT's exhortation.

A bracing beginning you offered, Wen, to the bicentennial celebration, which, may I suggest, focuses the question: What might be that radical response? Have we grasped, friends, the root of the problem-*challenge*-**opportunity** before us?

Your offering Sy (Montgomery) followed, upon being presented with the PEN New England Thoreau Prize for Nature Writing. I can envision still the picture you conjured up of your unexpected, and blessed, embrace of Athena (a veritable octopus) and the love that that embrace awoke in you for this fellow creature right up to her death... and beyond. How does the word from the scriptures go, Sy, an ever New Testament? "The earth" [and all her creatures) "moaneth and travaileth, waiting upon man?"

You took up the thread Chris (Lydon), as moderator of the afternoon Pen New England Round Table on Henry David's Literary Legacy with Deborah (Cramer), Jennifer (Haigh), John (Kaag), and Megan (Marshall), a spirited cast? The gems they offered were many and precious. How has that offering lived on in you, Chris? Upon reflection was the transcendental heart of that legacy addressed?

~~~

As with all the words that have been shared at this bicentennial celebration, this offering has been inspired by Henry David himself.

I begin, accordingly, with a further and related question, which I will go into at greater length toward the end of these words:

How aware are we of the source of Henry David's inspiration?

How aware, that is, are we of how alive Henry David, indeed, is? And, if this thought isn't just a figure of speech, figment of my imagination, how aware are we of what he who bore the earthly name Henry David Thoreau may be asking of us "Thoreauvians," of *We the People* today — as we speak?

'Twas the best of times and the worst of times" / The worst of times and the very best.

Timing…

Is there a more important consideration for us as Thoreauvians than to be truly present, present of mind?

~ ~ ~

I offer two related strands of this unfolding thread.

1) At an earlier annual meeting I attended, over a decade ago, one of the speakers was deeply concerned about the issue of global warming. Like Wen, his words were impassioned, and more. A life of quiet desperation?

After the speaker's talk, I was moved to go up to him and express my heartfelt appreciation for what he shared, how deeply the issue concerned him. He nodded, took a deep breath. I considered, went on, "The question that I take from your talk, bear in myself, is: How do we hold ourselves in such troubled and troubling times — where the cross-winds are many and mounting — *so as to receive the inspirations that can actually make a difference not only in our lives but in the world in which we find ourselves?*"

I was not sure if my words were clearly understood. Have you a sense, friends, of what I was seeking to say? Words from *Walden* return to heart and mind:

> *I learned this, at least, by my experiment; that if one advances confidently in the direction of his dreams, and endeavors to live the life which he has imagined, he will meet with a success unexpected in common hours. He will put some things behind, will pass an invisible boundary; new, universal, and more liberal laws will begin to establish themselves around and within him; or the old laws be expanded, and interpreted in his favor in a more liberal sense, and he will live with the license of a higher order of beings. In proportion as he simplifies his life, the laws of the universe will appear less complex and solitude will not be solitude, nor poverty poverty, nor weakness weakness. If you have built castles in the air, your work need not be lost; that is where they should be. Now put the foundations under them.*

As noted, we will pick up this strand of the thread at the end of the offering.

The second introductory thought:

2) We live in extraordinary times. If we are to be up to these times, do they not ask of us extra-ordinary efforts — in every thought, word, and deed. I speak of efforts that each of us can offer at any/every time and place. If, as expressed, we are present?

In this regard, who hasn't heard the story (not only of that old

Transcendental bug but) of the hurricane headed smack for the mainland... only to suddenly, unexpectedly veer off and exhaust itself out at sea... the tornado, twister that veers off into the "bush?"

What happened?

Might it be that thoughts (prayers and all) of those bracing for the impact were/are real, indeed as real as the very man-made civilization, itself, that has arisen out of nothing more or less than just that: our thoughts, designs, architectural plans?

I speak, friends, not in intellectual but *existential* terms — as I am sure a good number in this audience can appreciate. I speak of what may lie at the core of our very existence

~ ~ ~

The Thoreau We Do Not Yet Know?

I speak, friends, as a native son of Concord & founder of The Center for American Studies. As Thoreau noted in his "Reading" chapter of *Walden*: *"It is time we had uncommon schools; it is time that villages were universities.*

At the Center for American Studies, our village university/uncommon school, we do not offer talks, lectures, speeches, papers, but what we refer to as "offerings," offered up at best in, and out of, the present, the eternal present. As best we are able. Simply expressed, we invite those who are interested in taking part in our gatherings to speak to what lies deepest in their hearts.

So it is with this offering, which introduces a labor of love that has unfolded over the last three decades plus, entitled *"Says I to Myself"*: *Thoreau's Seminal Science of the Spirit.* The book, a kindred testament would do justice to words Henry David penned in his maiden voyage, *A Week on the Concord and Merrimack Rivers*: "The researcher is more memorable than the researched." Indeed, was not Heisenberg, himself, saying something akin to these very words?

"In most books," Henry David noted in the opening paragraphs of

Walden, "the I, or first person, is omitted; in this it will be retained; that, in respect to egotism, is the main difference. We commonly do not remember that it is, after all, always the first person that is speaking. I should not talk so much about myself if there were anybody else whom I knew as well. Unfortunately, I am confined to this theme by the narrowness of my experience. **Moreover, I, on my side, require of every writer, first or last, a simple and sincere account of his own life, and not merely what he has heard of other men's lives."** [Emphasis added]

This offering, as the book itself, *"Says I to Myself": Thoreau's Seminal Science of the Spirit,* is a *Thoreauvian* treatment of Thoreau. Simply expressed. That is, it is not merely an objective study of another man's life, but, if I've succeeded at this task, it is a subjective, that is a human, that is a universal testament to all our lives. A heartfelt word of thanks goes to Bob Baron of Fulcrum Publishers, who first recognized its possibilities.

For early on I realized that I cannot simply write *a b o u t* Thoreau, this old friend and fellow townsperson. That wouldn't work, for what I had envisioned. My task was to endeavor to write not just *out of* Henry David's spirit, but out of that greater Spirit still that inspired Concord's native son, that would inspire us all?

That is, I had to walk the talk, the path of which I speak, the path of knowledge that would lead the spirit in man to the Spirit in the universe. And, after 33 years I am still en route, doing so. The means are the ends in process, every step along the way...

~ ~ ~

So who is the Thoreau we do not yet know? And why may it be important that we, friends, come to know him, ever more deeply — above all in these times in which we find ourselves?

Before hearing from Henry David, himself, on this matter, I offer words from a kindred spirit, Albert Einstein, to set the stage:

> We must never relax our efforts to arouse in the people of the

world, and especially in their governments, an awareness of the unprecedented disaster, which they are **absolutely certain** to bring on themselves, unless there is a fundamental change in their attitude toward one another as well as in their concept of the future. The splitting of the atom has changed everything, save our mode of thinking and thus we drift toward an unparalleled catastrophe ... **We shall require a substantially new manner of thinking if mankind is to survive**. (emphasis added)

As I trust many of you recall, Einstein went on to note that we cannot solve a problem with the same thinking that created it in the first place." Indeed, to try to do so, the Father of Modern Science added, is **"insanity**.**"**

If Einstein's words are clear, let us hearken to Henry David, himself, in particular to a further, and related, passage from *A Week:*

> *I am not without hope that we may, even here and now, obtain some accurate information concerning that OTHER WORLD which the instinct of mankind has so long predicted. Indeed, all that we call poetry, is a particle of such information, accurate as far as it goes, though it be but to the confines of the truth.*
>
> *If we can reason so accurately, and with such wonderful confirmation of our reasoning, respecting so-called material objects and events infinitely removed beyond the range of our natural vision, so that the mind hesitates to trust its calculations even when they are confirmed by observation, why may not our speculations penetrate as far into the immaterial starry system, of which the former is but the outward and visible type?*
>
> *Surely, we are provided with senses as well fitted to penetrate the spaces of the real, the substantial, the eternal, as these outward are to penetrate the material universe.*

In this little discussed passage, Thoreau offers a unique insight into the heart of his striving: the qualitative science or science of the spirit that, I suggest, he is heralding on our shores.

That is, in the passage, Thoreau:

1) Attests to an "OTHER WORLD" immaterial/spiritual;

2) States that the "instinct" of mankind has long predicted such an "immaterial" world;

3) Confesses that he, himself, preserves the hope that we can "obtain some accurate information concerning that OTHER ["immaterial"] WORLD";

4) Suggests that poetry, "as far as it goes," provides intimations of such an "immaterial" WORLD;

5) Notes that we can "reason accurately" with respect to "so-called material objects and events infinitely removed beyond the range of our natural vision";

6) This being the case, Thoreau inquires why our reasoning may not "penetrate as far into the immaterial starry system";

7) Invites us to consider the possibility that (as water condenses into ice) the former, material world, "is but the outward and visible type" of the latter, "immaterial starry system," the world of the spirit;

The passage ends with the author's conviction that such a "hope" need not be in vain: "Surely, we are provided with senses as well fitted to penetrate the spaces of the real, the substantial, the eternal, as these outward are to penetrate the material universe."

What, in fact, is Henry David speaking about?

~ ~ ~

I have noticed that we have at this bicentennial celebration a good many friends among us from what was referred to in Henry David's day as the "orient."

With those from India, in particular, one find vestiges to this day of such "senses," such a "hope" — in the very middle, that is, of their foreheads. I refer to what is spoken of as the "third eye," chakra, or lotus flower. The terms bespeak an *inner* organ of perception that has become latent, fallen, so to speak, asleep.

For a reason.

Might that reason be so that we can *focus on* developing our *outer* organs of perception, beginning with the clear sight and those painstaking worldly calculations that are required to build the very man-made civilizations that we find ourselves in the midst of? So, this is, we can make sure that the roads, bridges, tunnels, skyscrapers, apartment buildings and high-rises stand up, as opposed to caving in on top of us?

The point being: in this worldly existence in which we find ourselves *precision* is required, painstaking calculations, as Henry David well understood — if, "thy kingdom come," we are to bring the heavens, the "New Jerusalem" itself, to earth. Even castles require foundations, as Concord's native son notes. I's must be dotted; t's crossed. For the old devil is, indeed, in the details. Angels, Archangels, and company, the "heavenly host" (if they, indeed, exist/are making a comeback) can divert our gazes, distract us from such worldly labors — if we're not on our toes. A stout soul one has to be to hold the balance, as Henry David himself recognized:

> *I perceive that I am dealt with by superior powers. This is a pleasure, a joy, an existence, which I have not procured myself. I speak as a witness on the stand, and tell what I have perceived.*
>
> *The morning and the evening were sweet to me, and I led a life aloof from society of men. I wondered if a mortal had ever known what I knew. I looked in books for some recognition of a kindred experience, but, strange to say, I found none. Indeed, I was slow to discover that other men had had this experience, for it had been possible to read books and to associate with men on other grounds. The maker of me was improving me. When I detected this interference I was profoundly moved. For years I marched as to a music in comparison with which the military music of the streets is noise and discord. I was daily intoxicated, and yet no man could call me intemperate. With all your science can you tell me how it is, and whence it is, that light comes into the soul?"*

What can one say?

Thoreau's life was, I suggest, dedicated to real-izing the existence that he was able to divine; that is to make such revelations his own; that is through such rigorous efforts to become truly free and in step with the Creation — as opposed to being "dealt with by superior powers." God bless them.

That is, Henry David strove to chart his own course in life. One, I suggest, that was devoted to the fulfillment of the hope of his being able to penetrate — consciously, freely, himself — "the spaces of the real, the substantial, the eternal." In this respect I speak of Henry David Thoreau as one of America's pioneering scientists of the spirit; I speak of his life as an aspiring labor of love.

What this labor, this fulfillment required was the blazing of that path of knowledge that, as expressed, leads the spirit in man to the Spirit in the universe. "Deep calls upon deep", Ralph Waldo Emerson intimates in his seminal book, *Nature*, "but in real life the marriage is not celebrated." "The Sage of Concord" penned these words in the 1830's.

And today...?

Wherein lies our possibilities for such a "marriage," union, re-union?

The life that Thoreau aspired to extended beyond what had come to be accepted as "reality" by many of his neighbors and fellow townspeople. Emerson continues: "There are innocent men who worship God after the tradition of their fathers, **but their sense of duty has not yet extended to the use of all of their faculties."** [emphasis added]

By "faculties" might Emerson be referring to the very senses of which Thoreau speaks as "well fitted to penetrate the spaces of [not just] the real, [but] the substantial, the eternal"?

"The Sage of Concord" goes on: "And there are patient naturalists, **but** [emphasis added] **they freeze their subject under the wintry light of the understanding**." The pendulum can also swing to the other extreme: a cold, faithless reason?

But... "But, when the faithful thinker, resolute to detach every object from personal [merely subjective] relations and see it in the light of thought [truly objectively, i.e. a revelation in and of itself] shall at the same time kindle science with the fire of the holiest affections, then will God go forth *anew* into the creation."

Imagine...

Can we? Will we?

Might Ralph Waldo Emerson be heralding not only his own aspiring path of knowledge, but that of his young friend, Henry David Thoreau, whose passage here on earth was an abbreviated one? Might such a path call for a honing and refining not only of our senses and sensibilities, but of our thinking, itself — allowing us, thereby, to, indeed, "divine" (and thereby *freely* unite with) those higher realms of which Concord's native son spoke?

~ ~ ~

How to put such considerations into perspective?

The physical sciences that have marked our age arose out of a religious or spiritual view of the universe with, some suggest, Galileo. In time the physical sciences themselves evolved on into the natural, social, and cognitive sciences.

Of note is the fact that each of these emerging disciplines, sciences had to fight against the biases of its predecessor — which, one after another, dismissed the emerging science as being "soft" or "pseudo" — before the emerging science came to be recognized as bonafide.

Of note is the fact that the natural, social, and cognitive sciences bear the distinct imprint — quantitative and reductionistic — of the physical sciences. As is so often the case, Thoreau addressed this critical point genially:

> *Science in many departments of natural history does not pretend to go beyond the shell, i.e., it does not get to animated nature at all. A history* [science] *of animated nature must itself*

be animated. Journal, March 20, 1858

The point is: this quantitative, reductionistic compulsion in modern science is nothing more than a modern, materialistic bias? Is it not? That is, science comes from the latin word "scientia," which means knowledge — not *that* knowing alone that is reduced to its mere quantitative, material expression, the lowest common denominator, its bare bones.

And the next step beyond the cognitive sciences?

With the splitting of the atom and the detonation of its bomb over Hiroshima and Nagasaki we, humanity, reached the depths, nadir: "the naked heap flesh and bones," humanity itself. Recognizing this fact, can we begin to raise our gazes anew, lift our visions?

Might it be time, friends, to speak — consciously/freely — of not just the *physical, natural, social* and *cognitive* sciences but of a fully realized *spiritual* science or science of the spirit? A reasoned faith, faithful reason: common sense?

In Emerson's completed masterwork, *The Natural History of the Intellect*, its middle chapters are entitled:

— **Imagination**/clear-seeing, clair-voyance. Earlier in this offering, we heard Thoreau speak to such a "sense." In his book *Nature* Emerson elaborates: "When reason is stimulated to more earnest vision, outlines and surfaces become transparent and are no longer seen. Causes and spirits are seen through them."

— **Inspiration**/clear hearing, clair-audience — the forces of the hearts, themselves vitalize our thinking.

— **Intuition or Common Sense/** clear sensing, clair-sentinence. The reference is to that 6th, 7th.... 11th, 12th sense that is common to us all, the revelation of our shared humanity. The devotion of our will imbues our thinking. It becomes engaged, vitalized, as opposed to merely abstract and theoretical. (Think with our heads, Henry David noted? No, no, we Americans think with/on our feet, "on the run," out of the fount of our will, ideally good will.)

Alcott gave voice to this final "promise," common sense, its essence, in his opening words, as Dean of the Concord School of Philosophy & Literature, but a good stone's throw down Lexington Road, on these very days in July of 1879, one hundred and thirty-eight years ago. In the words of an editor for the *Boston Journal:*

"Mr. Alcott, whose 10 lectures are to be on 'Christian Theism' then began in earnest the work of the summer by asking, 'What is expressed by each one of us, so far as we can explore our consciousness, when we say, 'I, myself'?"

That "promise" was summed up in the seven letters, comprising three words, (each word the same in sound) that, I believe, constitutes Emerson's *life* philosophy: *"I, Eye, Aye!* And, as we've heard, Thoreau honed this angle of vision with his own testimony: "'Says I to myself,' should be the motto of my journals."

Does the "promise," the secret, friends, becomes ever more manifest?

~ ~ ~

Says I to myself.... What/who are we speaking about?

In his 1986 Iona College Address, Stanley Cavell, a name known to many, I trust, a colleague, friend, and member in memoriam of The Center for American Studies Honorary Circle of Trustees, addressed this "promise":

> *"This is a most happy occasion for me, and I do not wish to mar it by speaking of unhappy things. But I will not belittle it by speaking of anything less than what matters most to me as a teacher and a writer and a citizen. One of these matters I share in common with every thinking person on earth, the imagination, or the refusal of imagination, of nuclear war, the most famous issue now before the world.*
>
> *Another matter is, in comparison, one of the most obscure issues of the world, and I share it, at most, with a few other obscure persons: the inability of our American culture to listen to the words, to possess them in common, of one of the founding*

> *thinkers of our culture, Ralph Waldo Emerson, an inability which presents itself to me as our refusal to listen to ourselves, to our own best thoughts. The particular odd matter I am moved to speak about by this occasion... is how this famous matter of destructiveness and this obscure matter of the repression of thinking have conjoined in my mind."*

In speaking of Emerson, I believe Stanley would agree that he is also speaking of Thoreau, of the "Genius" that is, of Concord. For its celebrated authors gave voice, each with his/her own accents and intonations, to that greater Cosmopolitan Spirit that united them all.

In the book, *Says I to Myself: Thoreau's Seminal Science of the Spirit*, I have spoken not just of knowledge but a p a t h of knowledge.

An overview of the steps on that path follow, that is the stages — if we can imagine — through which the soul passes in order to c o m e to know something, above all that which is not a thing but rather that which is living, alive. The knowing I speak of is not that of a steel trap. CLAP! "I've got it!" The knowledge spoken of is an *unfolding* revelation, as delicate, at times, as the blossom itself. Those steps, passages, are:

- I, An Awakening Sense of the Self
- Intimations of Kinship
- Dedication
- Wonder
- Reverence
- Sympathy
- Forgetting
- Self-Transformation -
- Correspondence
- Transcendence
- Knowing
- Re-creation

~ ~ ~

If the foregoing has made sense, I trust that the following point will as well. It brings us to the crux of the issue, as noted in the January 7, 1857 journal passage of Henry David Thoreau offered by a friend and kindred spirit, Nassir (Ghaemi):

> *All existence, all satisfaction and dissatisfaction, all event was symbolized in this way* [a dream]. *Now I seemed to be lying and tossing, perchance, on a horrible, a fatal rough surface, which must soon, indeed, put an end to my existence, though even in the dream I knew it to be the symbol merely of my misery; and then again, suddenly, I was lying on a delicious smooth surface, as of a summer sea, as of gossamer or down or softest plush, and life was such a luxury to live. My waking experience always has been and is such an alternate Rough and Smooth.* **In other words, it is Insanity and Sanity."** "*I am under an awful necessity,*" Henry David went on, "*to be what I am.*"

Can we relate, friends? Life is borne not just of smiles but of tears?

How, Nassir, do we face such "insanity," that which, hearkening back to Wen's opening words, some may speak of as "evil" on these shores? Is there is any more significant, more pressing issue for us, for humanity today?

Those who Henry David inspired, Gandhi, King, Chavez, among others, did so by taking seriously the words of an ever New Testament: "*Love your enemy; bless them that curse you; do good to them that hate you; and pray for them who despitefully use you and persecute you.*"

God bless such scoundrels (Trump, Hilary, if/as you insist), and keep them, *and let His light shine down upon them.*

Another speaker of, as noted, oriental (Indian) origin, James (Mathew), offered us an insight into this calling to love our enemy, as it affected Henry David's life. Specifically, the speaker contrasted Thoreau's defense of John Brown's use of violence, murder itself, the taking of others' lives, with Gandhi's view of the matter, in relationship, that is, to a related incident in India. Gandhi wrote:

> *I am prepared to die. But there is no cause for which I am prepared to kill. There is no escape for any of us save through truth and non-violence. I know that war is wrong, an unmitigated evil. I know too that it has to go. I firmly believe that freedom won through bloodshed or fraud is no true freedom... By making a dharma of violence we shall reap the fruits of our own actions.*

The appreciation I expressed to the speaker was accompanied by the question whether the taking of another's life was not a form of suicide. "An eye for an eye," the Mahatma noted, "makes the whole world blind." Do you feel, James, that you "offering" was heard, hearkened to?

[As this testament on Eternal Love has suggested, Henry David may have had not just a change of mind but a change of heart in this very, and most telling, respect: the appropriatenesses of the use of violence. Such a prospect brings into a more transcendent dimension an appreciation for the words: "live and learn."]

Concord's other celebrated author Nathaniel (Hawthorne) spoke to this matter of insanity, evil, with his characteristic incisiveness: "The unpardonable sin might consist in a want of love and reverence for the Human Soul."

The point of this strand of our thread, friends?

Might the souls who have "passed on," those we refer to as the dead, in fact, be more alive than to date we've imagined? Indeed, might they be with us, as we speak? That is, if brother John remained near and dear to Henry after their maiden voyage on the Concord and Merrimack Rivers, as Henry noted, lending him a hand along his way, might we be inspired to do the same? I speak not only of offering up our own best thoughts, but taking to heart whatever inspirations return to mind.

~ ~ ~

Drawing this offering toward its end, I would like to touch on the opening chord that Michael (Frederick) struck on Wednesday, a passage from Thoreau's "Paradise (to be) Regained," his Reform Papers:

> *"Love is the wind, the tide, the waves, the sunshine. Its power is incalculable; it is many horsepower. It never ceases, it never slacks; it can move the globe without a resting place; it can warm without fire; it can feed without meat; it can clothe without garments; it can shelter without roof; it can make a paradise within.... But though the wisest men in all ages have labored to publish this force, and every human heart is, sooner or later, more or less, made to feel it, yet how little is actually applied to social ends."*

Love... applied to social ends? Can you think of any more important consideration, friends?

This chord re-sounded toward the end of the gathering in the words you offered Terry (Tempest Williams): "Can we love ourselves and the world enough to change?... We lose nothing by loving. No one knew this more than Henry, love and loss."

Thank you, Terrie, for these words, simple and to the point. Brief as they are, can you say more, beginning with how you came to this central recognition — of love itself — about Concord's native son?

If we can hear such words, friends, Michael (Frederick), might we consider making them the theme of an upcoming annual gathering. I speak of Love, *redemptive* love, that "promise" which — might it be — blazes the trail for what has been referred to over the ages as "eternal love"?

I speak of love as *compassion, com-passion,* as a *suffering-with* the other. I do so for I believe, friends, that such love alone — as exemplified in the remarkable, archetypal story of the Peace Maker, the founder of the Iroquois Confederation — that such love provides us with the way *here on these shores* to deal with the "evil" and "insanity" that have been movingly addressed at this annual gathering. "Love your enemy..." Can we Thoreauvians, no less, imagine such an "incalculable power"?

In this respect, I bring greetings from two kindred spirits, modern day "knights," Dennis Kucinich and Bernard Lafayette. On the eve of his assassination, Dr. King gave Bernard the task of instituting non-violence globally. Dennis has striven to do just that through his undying effort to establish a Department of Peace, the *new* story. Both Dennis and Bernard can speak, movingly, to this theme of compassion/suffering-with, of redemptive/eternal love. Indeed, Dennis' response to the invitation was, as expected, a heartfelt one:

> *Dear Stuart, As ever, thank you for the invitation. If I am able to attend, I will. Currently I am scheduled to be out of the country, but that could change. Hope this finds you in good health and good spirits. Best wishes, Dennis*

~ ~ ~

Gathering the strands of our thread, I return to the opening question: "How do we hold ourselves in such troubled and troubling times — where the crosswinds are many and mounting — so as to receive, friends, the inspirations that can *actually* make a difference, not only in our own lives but in the world itself?" What is the stance that we're called to take?

If such questions are clear, Ronald, Deborah, Jayne and Phyllis (old friends), Theodore, Robert, Rebecca, Rochelle, Henrik, Paul and Michael — if such a question is clear to you as directors of the Thoreau Society, what kindred stance can you, friends, envision the society's work taking?

In considering such questions, a reflection comes to mind, one that addresses — might it be — the heart of the matter. Some speak of Transcendentalism as a movement. Others as a stillness. Truth be told, might Transcendentalism, in fact, be both — *in one*?

That is, the laws of grammar remind us that there is not only the active case (I wash my brother) and the passive case (I am washed by my brother), but there is also the reflexive case (I wash myself).

Reflexive...?

This third case is also referred to aptly as the "medium" case.

I invite you to consider the meaning of the word "medium." For it brings us, in turn, to a third friend and, I believe, kindred spirit of Henry David's. Alongside Thoreau, this third friend has inspired this offering, as well as the testament that stands behind it, *'Says I To Myself,' Thoreau's Seminal Science of the Spirit.*

This friend brought to civilization a renewed understanding of the reflexive, medium Transcendentalist stance, of the wisdom — if we can imagine? — of the middle. As Thoreau, Emerson, and Margaret Fuller in particular understood, Middle Europe's historic mission — all but destroyed by two world wars that raged on it soil — has been to balance the polarities of East (passive) and West (active), movement and stillness, the world of thought and that of actions... harmonized out of the mediating forces of the human heart.

I refer in this respect not just to Schiller, Fichte, Schelling and those representatives of the kindred German Idealistic stream, who were the subject of many of the offerings at The Concord School of Philosophy & Literature throughout that decisive decade of 1879-1888. An age, that is, that was ruled over by the spirit which *Harpers Magazine* referred to as "the genius of materialism." Nor do I refer to the "Master," Goethe himself, of whom Emerson spoke:

> *He has been one of the world's teachers and is to be for some time to come. The spirit and movement of an age are embodied in his books, and one reads with a growing reverence to every perusal of the mind that saw and has portrayed the world-spirit so well... The old eternal genius who built the world has confided himself more to this man [Goethe] than to any other... He has said the best things about nature that ever were spoken."*

Nor do I refer, friends, to the lesser known "ardent and holy Novalis," in Emerson's words. I speak of the young poet and mining engineer to whom Goethe, himself, looked up and who, upon commencing his studies in Leipzig, gave himself three mandates, mandates which Thoreau exemplified:

1. Know thyself in spirit;
2. Practice an aesthetic life in the soul;
3. Live invisibly in the body.

No, in these concluding words, I refer to and, thereby, invite more fully into our midst, our bicentennial celebration, another friend, Rudolf Steiner. Lesser known to many, this kindred spirit grasped, I believe, Henry David's genius in its essence. Filling out the *Harper's Magazine* passage about The Concord School of Philosophy & Literature: "At the time when Germany itself is overpowered by the influence of Mill, Spencer, and Darwin, and the genius of materialism is getting so strong a hold everywhere..." this friend of humanity, a young man his 18th year, all but on his own, took up the torch from Emerson, Thoreau, Bronson Alcott, Margaret Fuller and company in the same days in July of 1879 that these elder "divines" gathered — on earth as in the heavens — at the Concord School, its "Hillside Chapel." From the heartland, an embattled Middle Europe, this singular, solitary soul spanned the arc from the old world to the new, from Vienna to Concord. I return to Rudolf Steiner's words that opened this postscript, trusting that they have taken on a fuller meaning.

No, in these concluding words, I refer to and, thereby, invite more fully into our midst, our bicentennial celebration, another friend, Rudolf Steiner. Lesser known to many, this kindred spirit grasped, I believe, Henry David's genius in its essence. Filling out the *Harper's Magazine* passage about The Concord School of Philosophy & Literature: "At the time when Germany itself is overpowered by the influence of Mill, Spencer, and Darwin, and the genius of materialism is getting so strong a hold everywhere..." this friend of humanity, a young man his 18th year, took up the torch in the heartland, an embattled Middle Europe. In the very same days in July of 1879 that Emerson, Thoreau, Bronson Alcott, Margaret Fuller and these elder "divines" gathered — on earth as in the heavens — at the Concord School, its "Hillside Chapel," to address this singular, solitary soul company in the same days in July of 1879 that these elder "divines" gathered From the heartland, an embattled Middle Europe, this singular, solitary soul spanned the arc from the old world to the new, Vienna to Concord. Beginning with Rudolf Steiner, I drew this "offering" to its end with a number of passages that, I trust, have words that opened this postscript, trusting that they have grown in meaning:

"People say today: He is not a true scientist who does not determine observation and experiment quite logically; who does not pass from thought to thought in strict conformity with the correct methods that have evolved. If he does not do this, he is no genuine thinker. But, my dear friends, what if reality happens to be an artist and scorns our elaborate, dialectical and experimental methods? What if nature herself works according to artistic impulses? If it were so, human science, according to nature, would have to become artistic, for otherwise there would be no possibility of understanding nature."

~ ~ ~

This offering began with words of thanks; I am glad to end it with the same.

My final thanks go to this friend, whose life task began four years later in his 22nd year with his being invited to edit the "Master's," Goethe's qualitative scientific works — considered by Goethe himself to be even more significant than *Faust* and his literary masterpieces. Out of Goethe's qualitative science — artistic in its essence — this kindred spirit, Rudolf Steiner forged and brought into the world, civilization itself, a spiritual science, science of the spirit, that reasoned faith/faithful reason, *common* sense for which Henry David set a vital cornerstone here on the shores of our ever "New World."

Such a fully realized science reflects, I do believe, that medium case. It reflects that stance, which, when we take it to heart, is destined to bridge the chasm spoken of between East and West, movement and stillness, our lofty heads and laborious hands.

An introduction to friend Rudolf Steiner was granted me by the beloved Dutch doctor, Leen Mees, with whom I was granted the blessing to work on his own masterpiece, the book *Blessed by Illness*.

"When I first shook this friend's hand," Leen noted, "it was as though no one was there." The good doctor reflected, "Yet never before had I experienced so strongly my own presence." Leen's reflections deepened, "Rudolf Steiner was **totally** there for me."

A heartfelt thanks to this friend of humanity, who, in Thoreau's words, offered anew, and those of Emerson to follow, took up the torch — which we have devoted ourselves to kindling over this bicentennial celebration — and carried it on into our modern scientific age.

> *"I am not without hope that we may, even here and now, obtain some accurate information concerning that OTHER WORLD, which the instinct of mankind has so long predicted.* [Indeed] *If we can reason so accurately, and with such wonderful confirmation of our reasoning, respecting so-called material objects and events infinitely removed beyond the range of our natural vision, so that the mind hesitates to trust its calculations even when they are confirmed by observation, why may not our speculations penetrate as far into the immaterial starry system, of which the former is but the outward and visible type?"*

Imagine... can we, will we? Emerson goes on:

> *"The genius is the scientist or geographer for the super-sensible regions and will design a map for the new super-sensible areas."*

~ ~ ~

I conclude, friends, with an encompassing word of gratitude to all who have contributed to this bounteous bicentennial gathering — graced, as I've sought to express, by "the [illumined] shades of the great and good for company."

So it has been in my experience right down to this final refrain, drawn from Ralph Waldo Emerson's aspiring eulogy of his beloved "brother," Concord's native son. (Nobody knew how much I loved Henry... I did not know how much I loved Henry.) As this blessed tribute from "The Sage of Concord" began my contribution to Claire's and Henry David's labors of love, eternal love, Waldo's tribute draws this offering to its end:

> *There is a flower known to botanists, one of the same genus with our summer plant called "Life-Everlasting," a Gnaphalium like that, which grows on the most inaccessible cliffs of the Tyrolese mountains, where the chamois dare hardly venture, and which the hunter, tempted by its beauty, and by his love, (for it is immensely valued by the Swiss maidens,) climbs the cliffs to gather, and is sometimes found dead at the foot, with the flower in his hand. It is called by botanists the Gnaphalium leontopodium, but by the Swiss Edelweisse, which signifies Noble Purity.*
>
> *Thoreau seemed to me living in the hope to gather this plant, which belonged to him of right. The scale on which his studies proceeded was so large as to require longevity, and we were the less prepared for his sudden disappearance. The country knows not yet, or in the least part, how great a son it has lost. It seems an injury that he should leave in the midst his broken task, which none else can finish,—a kind of indignity to so noble a soul, that it should depart out of Nature before yet he has been really shown to his peers for what he is.*
>
> *But he, at least, is content. His soul was made for the noblest society; he had in a short life exhausted the capabilities of this world; wherever there is knowledge, wherever there is virtue, wherever there is beauty, he will find a home."*

~ ~ ~

www.ingramcontent.com/pod-product-compliance
Lightning Source LLC
Chambersburg PA
CBHW020951090426
42736CB00010B/1360